THE MONEY ILLUSION

By

IRVING FISHER

Professor of Economics,
Yale University

ISBN: 9781639230976

Printed: September 2021

Cover Art By: Paul Amid

Published and Distributed By:
Lushena Books
607 Country Club Drive, Unit E
Bensenville, IL 60106
www.lushenabks.com

ISBN: 9781639230976

THE MONEY ILLUSION

By
IRVING FISHER
Professor of Economics,
Yale University

New York · ADELPHI COMPANY · *Publishers*

FIRST PRINTING, JULY, 1928
SECOND PRINTING, SEPTEMBER, 1928
THIRD PRINTING, SEPTEMBER, 1929

To

OWEN D. YOUNG

PIONEER IN WORLD FINANCE

ACKNOWLEDGMENTS

So many persons, interested in the problems of unstable money, have done me the favor of reading a mimeographed draft of this book that I cannot adequately express my thanks for their many helpful suggestions. Their names follow:

Fred E. Ayer, Carl G. Barth, B. H. Beckhart, H. F. Boettler, Gladwin Bouton, H. B. Brougham, Harry Gunnison Brown, W. Randolph Burgess, Ellis Chadbourne, Lawrence Chamberlain, Edwin J. Clapp, J. M. Clark, Jack R. Crawford, Alfred M. Cressler, Miles M. Dawson, Paul H. Douglas, E. F. DuBrul, George W. Edwards, Clara Eliot, Herbert W. Fisher, Irving N. Fisher, William T. Foster, John P. Frey, Elisha M. Friedman, T. Alan Goldsborough, M. K. Graham, Hudson B. Hastings, E. W. Kemmerer, Robert D. Kent, Willford I. King, F. B. Knapp, Edwin W. Kopf, Vincent W. Lanfear, William C. Lee, David J. Lewis, Theron McCampbell, Lucia Ames Mead, Royal Meeker, Harry E. Miller, Wesley C. Mitchell, S. R. Noble, Robert W. Pomeroy, Emily F. Robbins, John E. Rovensky, A. W. Russell, Hugo Seaberg, George Shibley, Augustus Smith, Clyde H. Snook, Carl Snyder, George Soule, Edward W. Spooner, Darien A. Straw, H. C. Taylor, D. J. Tinnes, Robert H. Tucker, Kenneth S. VanStrum, H. M. Waite, H. A. Wallace, C. M.

Walsh, G. F. Warren, H. T. Warshow, Philip P. Wells, Ralph W. Wescott, Miriam E. West, H. Parker Willis, Robert B. Wolf, Frank A. Wolff, Harvey A. Wooster.

I give these names in alphabetical order, but I think none mentioned will feel that I am making invidious distinctions in emphasizing especially the help received from Professor B. H. Beckhart, Professor Harry Gunnison Brown, Dr. William T. Foster, Mr. M. K. Graham, Professor E. W. Kemmerer, Mr. Edwin W. Kopf, Dr. Royal Meeker, and Professor Miriam E. West.

PREFACE

This book is based on lectures given in the summer of 1927 before the Geneva School of International Studies.

Its aim is to show how unstable in buying power are all monetary units, including the dollar; what hidden causes produce that instability; what harm results, although ascribed to other causes; and what are the various remedies which have been tried or proposed. The purpose is not to propose any one remedy as the best but to put the problem to the reader, especially to the business reader.

For those who wish to pursue the subject further, a short reading list and other material are provided in the Supplement. All books mentioned in the text will also be found in this list.

IRVING FISHER

Yale University,
New Haven, Connecticut.

TABLE OF CONTENTS

CHAPTER I

CHAPTER II

CHAPTER III

CHAPTER IV

PAGE

CHAPTER V

CHAPTER VI

CHAPTER VII

CHAPTER VIII

SUPPLEMENT—HELPS FOR FURTHER STUDY

SECTION I

SECTION II

SECTION III

SECTION IV

THE MONEY ILLUSION

CHAPTER I

A GLANCE AT THE MONEY ILLUSION

INTRODUCTION

AS I write, your dollar is worth about 70 cents. This means 70 cents of pre-war buying power. In other words 70 cents would buy as much of all commodities in 1913 as 100 cents will buy at present. Your dollar now is not the dollar you knew before the War. The dollar seems always to be the same but it is always changing. It is unstable. So are the British pound, the French franc, the Italian lira, the German mark, and every other unit of money. Important problems grow out of this great fact —that units of money are not stable in buying power.

A new interest in these problems has been aroused by the recent upheavals in prices caused by the World War. This interest, nevertheless, is still confined largely to a few special students of economic conditions, while the general public scarcely yet know that such questions exist.

Why this oversight? Why is it that we have been so slow to take up these fundamental problems which are of vital concern to all people? It is because of the "Money Illusion"; that is, the failure to perceive that the dollar, or any other unit of money, expands or shrinks in value. We simply take it for granted that "a dollar is a dollar"—that "a franc is a franc," that all money is stable, just as centuries ago, before Copernicus, people took it for granted that this earth was stationary, that there was really such a fact as a sunrise or a sunset. We know now that sunrise and sunset are illusions produced by the rotation of the earth around its axis, and yet we still speak of, and even think of, the sun as rising and setting!

We need a somewhat similar change of ideas in thinking about money. Instead of thinking of a "high cost of living" as a rise in price of many separate commodities which simply happen, by coincidence, to rise at the same time, we shall find instead that it is really the dollar, or other money unit, which varies.

THE MONEY ILLUSION WITHIN YOUR COUNTRY

Almost every one is subject to the "Money Illusion" in respect to his own country's currency. This seems to him to be stationary while the money of other countries seems to change. It may seem strange but it is true that we see the rise or fall of foreign money better than we see that of our own.

For instance, after the War, we in America knew that the German mark had fallen, but very few Germans knew it. This was certainly true up to 1922 when with another economist (Professor Frederick W. Roman) I studied price changes in Europe. On my way to Germany I stopped in London and consulted with Lord D'Abernon, then British Ambassador to Germany. He said: "Professor Fisher, you will find that very few Germans think of the mark as having fallen." I said: "That seems incredible. Every schoolboy in the United States knows it." But I found he was right. The Germans thought of commodities as rising and thought of the American gold dollar as rising. They thought we had somehow cornered the gold of the world and were charging an outrageous price for it. But to them the mark was all the time the same mark. They lived and breathed and had their being in an atmosphere of marks, just as we in America live and breathe and have our being in an atmosphere of dollars. Professor

Roman and I talked at length with twenty-four men and women whom we met by chance in our travels in Germany. Among these only one had any idea that the mark had changed.

Of course, all the others knew that prices had risen, but it never occurred to them that this rise had anything to do with the mark. They tried to explain it by the "supply and demand" of other goods; by the blockade; by the destruction wrought by the War; by the American hoard of gold; by all manner of other things,—exactly as in America when, a few years ago, we ourselves talked about the "high cost of living," we seldom heard anybody say that a change in the dollar had anything to do with it.

I remember particularly a long talk with one very intelligent German woman who kept a shop in the outskirts of Berlin. She gave all kinds of trivial reasons for the high prices. There was a grain of truth in some of them, just as there is a grain of truth in the idea that a small part of the seeming motion of the stars is real. But the main fact of the tremendous increase in the volume of "marks" and of the action of this paper money inflation on prices was not even glimpsed by the German shop woman. For eight years she had been victimized by the changing mark but had never once suspected the true cause—inflation. When I talked with her the inflation had gone on until the mark had depreciated by more than ninety-eight per cent, so that it was only a fiftieth of its original value (that is, the price level had risen about fifty fold), and yet she had not been aware of what had really happened. Fearing to be thought a profiteer, she said: "That shirt I sold you will cost me just as much to replace as I am charging you." Before I could ask her why, then, she sold it at so low a price, she continued: "But I have made a profit on that shirt because I bought it for less."

She had made no profit; she had made a loss. She *thought* she had made a profit only because she was deceived by the "Money Illusion." She had assumed that the marks she had paid for the shirt a year ago were the same sort of marks as the marks I was paying her, just as, in America, we assume that the dollar is the same at one time as another. She had kept her accounts in what was in reality a fluctuating unit, the mark. In terms of this changing unit her accounts did indeed show a profit; but if she had translated her accounts into dollars, they would have shown a large loss, and if she had translated them into units of commodities in general she would have shown a still larger loss—because the dollar, too, had fallen.

Chart I shows her apparent gain and actual loss.

We found the same complacent assumption of stability in other countries. Austrians, Italians, French, English,—all peoples assumed that their own respective moneys had not fallen in value, but that goods had risen.

WHEN TWO COUNTRIES COMPARE NOTES

It follows, of course, that when people from different countries with different moneys compare notes they find that their ideas are in conflict. This is well illustrated by the case of an American woman who owed money on a mortgage in Germany. The World War came and she had no communication with Germany for two years. After the War she visited Germany, intending to pay the mortgage. She had always thought of it as a debt of $7,000. It was legally a debt of 28,000 marks, in terms of German money. She went to the banker who had the matter in charge and said: "I want to pay that mortgage of $7,000." He replied: "The amount isn't $7,000; it is 28,000 marks; that sum today

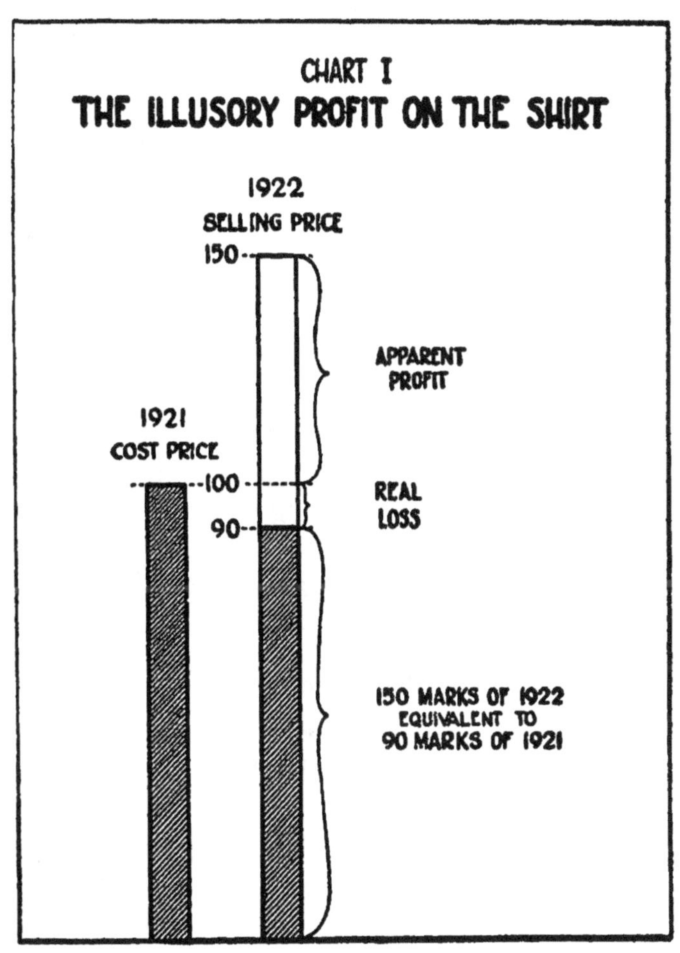
CHART I
THE ILLUSORY PROFIT ON THE SHIRT
1922
SELLING PRICE
150
1921
COST PRICE
100
90
APPARENT
PROFIT
REAL
LOSS
150 MARKS OF 1922
EQUIVALENT TO
90 MARKS OF 1921

is about $250." She said: "Oh! I am not going to take advantage of the fall of the mark. I insist upon paying the $7,000." The banker could not see the point; he showed that legally this was not necessary and he could not understand her scruples. As a matter of fact, however, she herself failed to take account of a corresponding, though lesser, change in the dollar. She was thinking in terms of American dollars, just as the banker was thinking in terms of German marks. She insisted on paying $7,000 instead of paying $250, but she would have rebelled if she had been told that the dollar also had fallen, that the equivalent in buying power of the original debt was not $7,000, but $12,000, and that she ought, therefore, to pay $12,000! Then *she* would not have seen the point!

THE MONEY ILLUSION IN AMERICA

Thus, we Americans are no exception in regard to the "Money Illusion." An American is quite lost if he tries to think of the dollar as varying. He cannot easily think of anything by which to measure it. Even with our gold standard we have a dollar fluctuating in buying power. Yet we think of the dollar as fixed. It is fixed only in the sense that it is redeemable in a fixed number of grains of gold. It is not fixed in the amount of goods and benefits it can command.

A very able American business man said to me some years ago: "I have made a great deal of money and I have been on the boards of directors of a great many concerns. I haven't before heard anyone talk about an unstable dollar as having anything to do with hard times; I take no stock in any such idea."

It is refreshing to note, however, that many far-sighted business men are now aware of the changeableness of the dollar. In 1925, at a time when people were marvelling at how high the stock market seemed, Secretary Mellon pointed out that, if we took account of the depreciated dollar, prices on the stock market really were not so high as they had been before the War. He was right; for a depreciated dollar tends to raise prices of commodities and property in general, including stocks representing shares in property.

Earlier in the same year, Mr. James H. Rand, Jr., now President of Remington Rand Inc., had pointed out in some detail the same fact.

Having been interested for a long time in this subject of the fluctuating dollar, he had, from time to time, kept two accounts, one in actual prices, the other translated into such prices as would have prevailed if the dollar had remained stable in buying power. This he did to make sure that he was not being victimized, like the shop woman in Berlin, by unstable money. Without such a translation into actual buying power, we are all likely to deceive ourselves.

In 1919, which was in a period of inflation, a leading banker learned, for the first time, of translating accounts into stable dollar values. When he saw the point, he took a pad out of his pocket and made some calculations. Then he exclaimed: "I have been boasting about how my bank has expanded its deposits and loans. But now I see, when I take into account the depreciated dollar, that I am only doing about the same business as before the War at twice the old level of prices. The expansion of which I have been boasting has been an illusion."

The United States Steel Corporation has the reputation of having grown rapidly—and it has grown very rapidly; but its growth seems to be more than it is because in comparing the company's present and past records the depreciation of the dollar is overlooked. This comparison of real with seeming growth has been made in detail by Mr. Ernest F. DuBrul in a pamphlet mentioned in the Supplement.

APPLICATION TO INVESTORS

Apply the idea of the unstable dollar to your own case. Suppose that you received before the War a dividend of four dollars per share, and that now you are receiving five dollars per share. Perhaps you cherish the idea that your dividend is now twenty-five per cent more than it used to be. But when you consider what your dividend dollar will buy, you will find that the real return to you is actually 12½ per cent less!

Work it out and see. The dollar of today, as compared with the dollar of 1913, is worth about 70 pre-war cents, as already mentioned; that is, it will buy about seventy per cent as much goods, on the average, as the dollar of 1913 bought. Using this figure, suppose you translate your five dollar dividend of today back into the old 1913 dollars. Since each of these five present-day dollars is really only 70 cents, of pre-war standard, you will find that you actually have only five times 70 cents, or three dollars and a half, of pre-war standard. You used to get four dollars in your dividend and now you are getting only three dollars and a half of the same standard of buying power.

Two investigators in the banking and brokerage business have recently shown what this means to the American investor, and have published their findings in two excellent books: Edgar Lawrence Smith's "Common Stocks as Long Term Investments" and Kenneth Van Strum's "Investing in Purchasing Power." Both of these men, working by independent methods, have startled many conservative investors by showing that the bondholder does not necessarily have a safe investment, as measured in buying power, even in this country. The reason is simple. As long as a dollar is not safe, any agreement to pay a dollar is not safe. However certain it may be that you are going to get the promised dollar, it is not at all sure what the dollar is going to be worth when you get it. These investigators have found that, on some occasions, the bondholder, instead of getting interest, was really taking a loss in terms of real buying power. He was actually losing part of his principal; but, like the German shopkeeper, he did not know it.

IS GOLD STABLE?

The Money Illusion is strong even in countries which have lost the gold standard and are on a paper money basis, despite two reminders which business men have before their eyes. These are the ever-changing quotations of their former gold money—mark, franc, crown or whatever—and the ever-changing quotations of foreign moneys. But stronger yet is the Money Illusion in gold standard countries, where these two reminders are absent. In fact their absence is often pointed to, with pride, as proof that the money is sound and stable.

One form of such "proof" of this stability is that the "price of gold" never varies in a gold standard country. In the United States pure gold sells at about twenty dollars an ounce (exactly $20.67) and has remained at that fixed price ever since 1837 when the pure gold content of the dollar was fixed at about one-twentieth of an ounce (exactly 23.22 grains) of pure gold. Of course the two figures mutually imply each other and afford absolutely no evidence that gold is constant in its buying power over other commodities. They merely mean that gold is constant in terms of gold.

I once jokingly asked my dentist—at a time when people were complaining about "the high cost of living"—whether the cost of gold for dentistry had risen. To my surprise he took me seriously and sent his clerk to look up the figures. She returned and said: "Doctor, you are paying the same price for your gold that you always have."

Turning to me the dentist said: "Isn't that surprising? Gold must be a very steady commodity."

"It's exactly as surprising," I said, "as that a quart of milk is always worth two pints of milk."

"I don't understand," he said.

"Well, what is a dollar?" I asked.

"I don't know," he replied.

"That's the trouble," I said. "The dollar is approximately one-twentieth of an ounce; there are, therefore, twenty dollars in an ounce of gold, and naturally an ounce of gold must be worth $20. The dollar is a unit of weight, just as truly as the ounce. It is a unit of weight masquerading as a stable unit of value, or buying power."

CONCLUSION

Our fixed-weight dollar is as poor a substitute for a really stable dollar as would be a fixed weight of copper, a fixed yardage of carpet, or a fixed number of eggs. If we were to define a dollar as a dozen eggs, thenceforth the price of eggs would necessarily and always be a dollar a dozen. Nevertheless, the supply and demand of eggs would keep on working. For instance, if the hens failed to lay, the price of eggs would not rise but the price of almost everything else would fall. One egg would buy more than before. Yet, because of the Money Illusion, we would not even suspect the hens of causing low prices and hard times.

In what sense, then, should a dollar be fixed, if not in weight? Evidently, in buying power. We use a dollar as a unit of value, or buying power, not as a unit of weight. We have other units of weight, the pound, ounce, grain, gram. We use these units of weights for weighing. But the dollar is a unit of weight never used for weighing. 23.22 grains of silver or copper is not a dollar. Only 23.22 grains of gold is a dollar and even then, while the grain means to us weight, the dollar does not. We never think of it in any such way. We think of it as a unit of value. No one cares, or should care, what a dollar weighs. What it buys is the vital question. As an economist, General F. A. Walker, said, "money is as money does" or "the dollar is what the dollar buys." To confuse the fixed weight of the dollar with a fixed value is like confusing a fixed weight of a yardstick with a fixed length. If the Bureau of Standards should put out yardsticks always weighing the same, that would not insure their having the same length. They could be used accurately for weighing sugar but not, with any great accuracy, for measuring cloth.

It follows that our dollar could be used accurately for weighing sugar, but it cannot at present be used, with accuracy, for measuring value. This fact nevertheless is hidden from us by the Money Illusion.

CHAPTER II

EXTENT OF MONEY FLUCTUATION

THE INDEX NUMBER

WE have seen that, in spite of the popular belief to the contrary, the dollar or franc, or other monetary unit, unlike other units of measure, is very far from constant. But how can we tell when the value of the dollar has changed and how much it has changed? By what means can we measure our money in terms of *real* value? The answer is, by means of Index Numbers or, for short, Indexes.

An Index is a figure which shows the average percentage change in the prices of a number of representative goods from one point of time to another.

Suppose we start with a dollar's worth of goods in 1913, a market basket containing all sorts of representative goods—bread, butter, eggs, milk, cloth and so on, in the proportions in which they were traded in, and such that the whole assortment could be bought in 1913 for one dollar.

Then let us suppose that, while the 1913 dollar would buy that market basketful, the dollar of 1919 would buy only half of it. That is, the price of that basket in 1919 was two dollars instead of one dollar; the goods in the basket, taken all together, had doubled in price. It follows, according to these figures, that the 1919 index number of commodity prices is twice the 1913 level; that is, it is 200, if we take 100 as the price level of 1913.

This statement does not, of course, mean that every one of the goods had doubled in price. Some kinds of goods had more than doubled in price and some had less than doubled; a few even had fallen.

Such a doubling of prices, on the average, did actually occur between 1913 and 1919. We can express it in either of two ways. We may say that the price index, or price of the assortment of goods in the imaginary basket, was doubled, or we may say that the dollar was worth half as much.

Today the value of the dollar is higher than in 1919; it will buy more than two-thirds of the market basket which cost a dollar in 1913. That is, as before stated, today's dollar is worth about 70 pre-war cents.

As already said, the market basket is supposed to contain the various commodities in their right proportions. But, in actual practice, it usually makes very little difference whether the proportions are carefully chosen or not. This is partly because most of the commodities usually go up and down in sympathy and partly for other reasons. But of the fact there is no question, surprising as it may seem to those not familiar with index numbers. Chart II constructed from the figures published in Bulletin 181 of the United States Bureau of Labor Statistics illustrates two curves, one curve "weighted," according to the amounts bought and sold, the other "unweighted," giving equal weight to each and every commodity. The reader can see for himself that usually the two curves move up and down together.

The United States Bureau of Labor Statistics publishes monthly an index based on the wholesale prices of 550 commodities. I publish one weekly based on 120 commodities. Carl Snyder, economist of the Federal Reserve Bank of New York, has constructed a general index, compiled

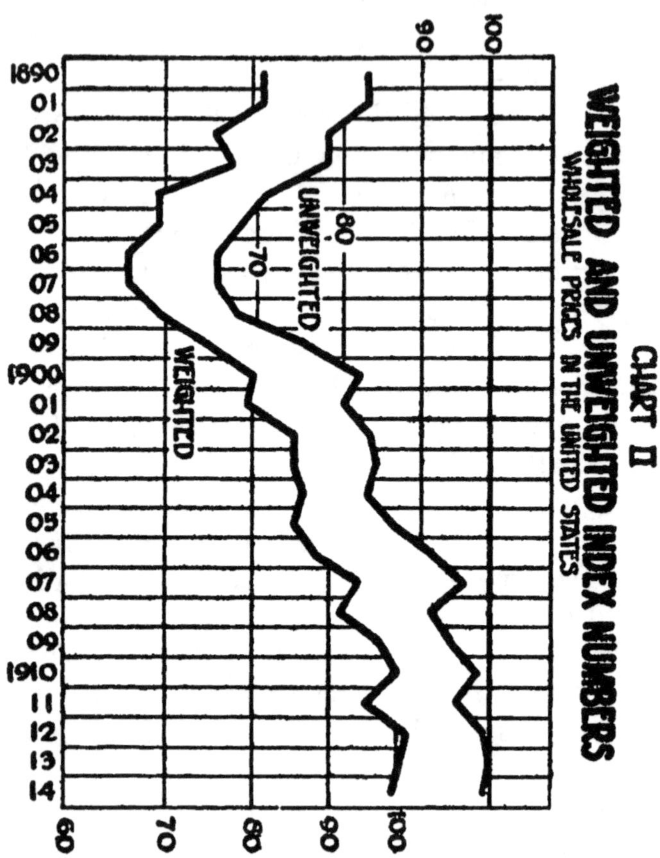

from the prices of goods, property and services of all descriptions, not only commodities, wholesale and retail, but stocks, bonds, real estate, wages, rents, and freights.

Indexes are increasingly used by statisticians, by the statistical departments of banks, by business men, and, in recent years, even by the general public. A number of commercial houses and some official agencies have adjusted wages by an index of the cost of living. The Dawes Plan for Germany's reparation payments makes some use of index numbers. The World Economic Conference at Geneva, in 1927, recommended that various kinds of indexes be constructed for world-wide use.

As already implied, if we, so to speak, turn an index of prices upside down, we get an index of the buying power of the dollar. The two indexes play see-saw with each other, one going up or down as the other goes down or up. So there are always these two indexes, one of prices and the other of the buying power of the dollar. Both tell us the same story but in opposite ways.

FLUCTUATIONS IN EUROPE

When we apply this instrument, the index, to the facts of history, what do we find has happened to price levels and money? Indexes show that the German commodity price level rose during, and following, the World War more than a trillion fold as compared with the level of the year 1913, or, to reverse the index, that the buying power of the German mark was reduced to less than one-trillionth part of what it was in 1913. In Russia the rise of prices was far less, yet it was over a billion fold. In Poland the rise was again far less; yet it was over a million fold. In Austria the rise was still less; yet it was twenty thousand fold. In Italy and France and several other countries it was still less; yet it was five to ten fold. In England, Canada, and in the United States it was still less; yet it was two to three fold; that is, the dollar and the pound fell to a half or a third of their pre-war buying powers.

FLUCTUATIONS IN AMERICA

During the Civil War the dollar fell rapidly, so that in 1865 its buying power was only two-fifths of that of 1860. Next, the dollar's buying power rose again until it was multiplied four fold in the 31 years between 1865 and 1896. Once more the tide turned and the dollar fell until its buying power in 1920 was only one-fourth what it had been in 1896. Finally, from May 1920 to June 1921 the dollar again rose rapidly in buying power, from 40 to 70 pre-war cents. All these figures are based on wholesale prices. If other sorts of prices are included the extreme fluctuations are reduced. Since 1921 the dollar has remained fairly stable, with comparatively minor changes, up to the present time.

Chart III shows what the dollar was worth in various years, five years apart, beginning with 1850. All figures are in terms of "pre-war cents," that is, 1913 cents.

These facts show that, while the changes in our dollar are small compared with the extreme changes in the German mark or in the Russian ruble, they have nevertheless been very great. An expansion in the dollar's worth of nearly four fold within a generation, an equal shrinkage within a still shorter time, followed by another great expansion in a little more than a year, show that our dollar has been far from stable. That is to say, even in the United States, a gold standard country, money changed in buying power just as truly, even if not as much, as it did in the paper standard countries.

DIFFERENT INDEXES AGREE

The indexes used in Chart III are made from wholesale prices but the results will not be far different if we use an index made from retail prices, or even one from "general" prices—of

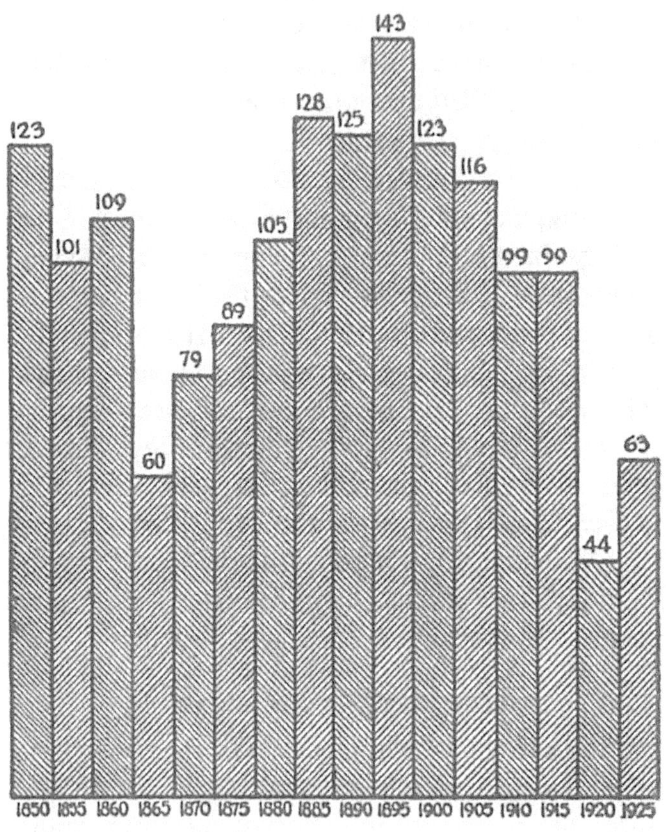
CHART III
BUYING POWER OF THE DOLLAR
IN 1913 CENTS
123
101
109
60
79
89
105
128
125
143
123
116
99
99
44
63
1850
1855
1860
1865
1870
1875
1880
1885
1890
1895
1900
1905
1910
1915
1920
1925

goods and services of all descriptions. Discrepancies between the wholesale index and the general index are shown in the accompanying table. It is interesting to see how closely these different indexes agree. The wholesale figures are repeated from Chart III. The general index, given in the last column, is that calculated by Carl Snyder.

Buying Power of the Dollar
in 1913 cents

	Wholesale	General
1875	89	88
1880	105	102
1885	128	122
1890	125	122
1895	143	145
1900	123	122
1905	116	116
1910	99	104
1915	99	97
1920	44	52
1925	63	59

The differences are, successively: 1, 3, 6, 3, 2, 1, 0, 5, 2, 8, 4 cents. The greatest difference is 8 cents (52–44 for 1920) the average difference is 3.2 cents and there are only two cases out of the eleven over 5 cents.

While it is a highly technical question what is the very best index or indexes to be used to guide stabilization the facts prove that even at the worst, as shown in this table, the various available indexes agree with each other fairly well. Each one shows an extremely variable dollar.

COMMENTS

What would we say if our yardstick, pound avoirdupois, bushel basket, gallon, or kilowatt were to shrink and swell—nearly four fold—back and forth? Suppose that a railway company were to order railway ties six feet long and that the foot rule were to quadruple in length before the time they were delivered! Or suppose that a grain elevator were to buy 1000 bushels of wheat, but the bushel basket meanwhile were to shrink to one-fourth its original size! Our dollar, the measure of value, nevertheless changes as the yardstick might if it were a rubber band, or as the pound might if the standard pound weight were made of something that takes up moisture from the air and afterward dries out again.

The reason the World War aroused us a little to the importance of this subject of unstable money was that it made almost all moneys in the world far more unstable than they had ever been before. Yet it required, in Germany for instance, a change of over a hundred fold occurring within the period of a few years to make any large number of people realize that there had been any change at all, so difficult is it to rid ourselves of the Money Illusion.

Even under such extreme conditions, the Money Illusion did not end. The idea of the stability of money was merely transferred by the Germans from their money to ours. Like a passenger who discovers, to his surprise, that his train is moving and not the one on the next track, the ordinary German, after the German price level had risen some hundreds of times, suddenly realized that the mark was falling and immediately assumed that the Swiss franc, or the American dollar, was stationary. It was then that the general public began, for the first time, to watch daily the foreign exchanges and promptly to adjust their own prices accordingly. They envied the foreigner for having what they now falsely assumed was a stable money. One result was a desire to "get back" to such a gold standard themselves; that any standard still better might be obtained was an idea never thought of. Thus the very instability of the paper mark, as soon as discovered, blinded them to the instability of the gold standard. The fact that gold was so very much more stable than unregulated paper money caused it to be idealized. But it is not, and never has been, ideal—far from it,—as the indexes just quoted clearly show.

CHAPTER III

WHY DOES MONEY FLUCTUATE?

CIRCULATION OF MONEY AND GOODS

THE question now arises *why* does money thus change in its buying power? The answer, in brief, is "*relative* inflation and deflation." The emphasized word "relative" means inflation or deflation relative to the volume of trade in any given period.

The term "money," as here used, includes three chief kinds: first, gold, into which all other money is convertible as long as the gold standard is maintained; second, paper money; and third, bank deposits,—the money we keep on deposit in banks and which is transferred by means of checks. These bank deposits, or "deposit currency" as they are often called, differ from paper money and gold money in acceptability. Gold and paper money are accepted by everyone without question. But a check on a bank is not accepted except by the individual consent of the person receiving it.

This deposit currency is much more important than the gold or paper money, because it does much more work in exchanging goods—in fact, eight or ten times as much.

Every time anyone buys anything of anybody, money, one of these three kinds, flows from the buyer to the seller, while the goods flow from the seller to the buyer. If now we add together all such flows of money in society as a whole, in the course of, say, a year, we get the total amount of money paid or circulated. In the course of a year in the United States, the money circulated adds up to approximately between 600 and 1000 billion dollars, say 900 billions of dollars. Since the total "money" in existence (including credit) is only about 30 billions, this must turn over about 30 times a year in order to do its necessary work in the nation's business of transferring goods from owner to owner.

To illustrate roughly, suppose taken together these goods all make up 30 billion tons circulated per year. These 30 billion tons, the entire goods stream, sold at $30 a ton on the average, make the 900 billion dollars' worth required to match the opposite money stream of 900 billion dollars.

RELATIVE INFLATION AND DEFLATION

If these two opposite flows, namely the circulation of money and the circulation of goods, each 900 billions of dollars in value, should keep going on at the same even pace, year after year, there would be no inflation and no deflation—and there could be no change in the general level of prices. Nor could there be any change in the general level of prices if these two streams were both to grow greater *at the same rate,* nor if they were both to grow less *at the same rate.*

This situation, where money and goods run along together, or their streams ebb and flow alike, may be called the "normal" one. That is, the flow of money, to accommodate business, keeps pace with the growth or shrinkage of business. That is what is meant by an "elastic currency."

But what if the two circulations do not thus keep pace? For instance, suppose that the circulation of goods remains the same year after year (say at 30 billion tons) but that the circulation of money increases (say to 1200 billion dollars). Then evidently the price level could not remain the same (at $30 a ton); otherwise the value of the goods stream would still be only 900 billion dollars instead of the 1200 which it must be to equal the circulation of money.

In short if more money pays for the same goods their price must rise, just as if more butter is spread over the same slice of bread it must be spread thicker, the thickness representing the price level, the bread the quantity of goods.

Next, suppose again that the circulation of goods remains the same but that the circulation of money decreases,—then the price level will fall. If less butter is spread over the same slice, it will have to be on the average thinner.

Next, suppose the circulation of money to remain constant, while the circulation of goods increases. The price level will fall; the same butter spread on a larger slice will be thinner.

Finally, suppose again the circulation of money to remain constant while that of goods decreases. The price level will rise; the same butter spread on a smaller slice will be thicker.

In fact, of course, we never find either of the two circulations staying constant. The circulation of goods is almost always increasing year by year, and usually at a fairly steady rate. The circulation of money also usually increases, although very unsteadily, and sometimes it actually decreases. But, whatever happens, the only important fact, *in so far as the price level is concerned,* is the *relation* between these two circulations.

We may, accordingly, include all four of the preceding cases, as well as all other possible cases, by saying: If the circulation of money increases *relatively* to the circulation of goods, the price level will rise. If, on the contrary, it decreases *relatively,* the price level will fall; that is, whether the butter is thick or thin depends on whether there is much or little butter *relatively* to the bread. In the first case, there is *relative* inflation; in the second, *relative* deflation; and the index of prices reveals from time to time which of the two is going on.

REAL INCOME

But, of course, *relative* inflation or deflation is not the whole story. Although, for the purpose of explaining a change in the general level of prices and the corresponding opposite change in the buying power of the dollar, it makes no difference whether the relative inflation or deflation is caused by a change in one or in the other or by a change in both of the two circulations, nevertheless it does make a difference for certain other purposes, including some questions of human welfare to be considered in later chapters.

Now, the human significance of money to any person depends principally on two things: (1) how many dollars of income he gets; and (2) what each of those dollars will buy. His real income is the product of these two factors. It is the buying power of one dollar multiplied by the number of dollars of his income; that is, it is the buying power of that income taken as a whole.

A man's real income is of supreme economic importance to him. Whether the real income of the average man increases or decreases depends, of course, on whether the total real income of society increases faster or slower than does the population. The real income per capita is the chief economic fact in any country.

THE TWO CIRCULATIONS PER CAPITA

Now, real income will expand or contract in proportion (approximately) to the circulation of goods. Consequently an increase or decrease in real income per capita is indicated by an increase or decrease in the circulation of goods per capita. In short, we may think of the circulation of goods per capita as a practical tell-tale of economic wellbeing per capita.

If we put also the flow of money on a per capita basis we can always apportion the cause of a rise or fall of the price level between money and goods. We can, for instance, say: If the flow of goods per capita remains the same, any change in the price level is due entirely to a change in the flow of money. If the flow of money per capita remains the same any change in the price level is due to a change in the flow of goods. If both flows per capita change, both are responsible for the change in the price level and in proportion to their respective changes.

For instance, if the per capita flow of money should double and the per capita flow of goods should be halved, each of these causes would double the price level. Each would have the same influence as the other; together they would increase the price level four fold.

ABSOLUTE INFLATION AND DEFLATION

The result of this way of stating the problem is that we may reduce to four the possible causes of changes in the general level of prices:

1. per capita increase of money circulated
2. " " decrease of money "
3. " " increase of goods "
4. " " decrease of goods "

The first two may be called "absolute inflation" and "absolute deflation" in contrast with "relative inflation" and "relative deflation" as already defined (which might also be described as the increase and decrease in the per capita flow of money relative to the per capita flow of goods).

By these definitions we have given precise meanings to the terms relative inflation, relative deflation, absolute inflation, absolute deflation. These will help us think clearly, instead of being contented with the vague meanings of "inflation" and "deflation" as commonly used.

MONEY DOMINATES

Most people have the idea that the last two of our four causes are the important ones,—that when the price level rises the rise is due wholly or chiefly to an actual scarcity of the individual goods concerned, and that, when the price level falls, the fall is due wholly or chiefly to an actual superabundance of the individual goods concerned. In other words, the common impression is that a high price level, a so-called "high cost of living," is not usually due to any absolute inflation (even if we do have to call it relative inflation according to our definition); and that a low price level is not usually due to any absolute deflation (even if we do have to call it relative deflation by our definition).

But there is no justification whatever for such ideas; they are chiefly due to our old friend the Money Illusion which hides from us the money side of the market, so that we look only at the goods side,—usually the wrong side to look at.

As a matter of historical fact, we seldom, if ever, find a case of noteworthy inflation or deflation which is not both relative and absolute. The money stream is found to vary greatly, while the goods stream varies comparatively little, especially per capita, that is, in relation to population. There is usually a slow and steady increase of the stream of goods per capita. The facts justifying this statement are given in the writings of various economists, including Professor Cassel of Sweden, Professor Keynes of

England, Professor Holbrook Working of California, and many others, including myself.

That changes in the money stream have been of overwhelming importance will not be questioned, of course, in such extreme cases as in the recent inflation and deflation in Germany, Russia, Poland, and Austria. Whatever may have been the facts as to the stream of goods, certainly the stream of money varied infinitely more. When the price level soars a thousand or a million fold, the rise is most certainly almost wholly due to inflation, and that inflation is both relative and absolute.

The same was undoubtedly true of the paper money of the French Revolution. It was true of the "Continental" paper money of our American Revolution, and of the "greenbacks" of our Civil War. So great was the depreciation during the American Revolution that even to this day, after a century and a half, we have an echo of it in the familiar phrase: "It isn't worth a Continental."

It is not so generally understood, however, that there is this same overwhelming importance of the changes in the money stream even in times of peace, and even in gold standard countries like the United States.

TEN AMERICAN EXAMPLES

In each of the following instances, covering all the important illustrations available in the United States, the inflation or deflation was both absolute and relative, and was each time the dominant factor in raising or lowering the price level:

(1) *Inflation,* 1849–1860. Gold gushed from California and Australia.

(2) *Further Inflation,* 1860–1865. During the Civil War the "greenbacks" were issued in increasing numbers.

(3) *Deflation,* 1865–1879. After the Civil War the "greenbacks" were reduced in number and finally made redeemable in gold.

(4) *Further Deflation,* 1879–1896. Gold mining tended to fall off while, at the same time, there was a "scramble for gold" among many nations then changing over from the "bimetallic" standard, which used both gold and silver, to the single gold standard.

This last period is especially interesting because it is the only period which, to many economists, seemed an exception to the rule. As one of those economists, I myself supposed, until recently, that there was, during these years, such a marked increase in the goods circulation as largely to explain the fall in the price level, even if the money circulation had increased as fast as the population increased. Books have been written to support this idea. But the recent studies of the goods stream—as revealed by the statistics of the physical volume of *production* given by Carl Snyder and Willford I. King, show that the goods circulation, or volume of trade, did not even increase as fast as the population. Snyder's figures show an increase in production from 1879 to 1896 of only 30 per cent, while population increased 44 per cent. It follows that if the money flow had increased exactly as fast as population, that is if the per capita flow of money had remained constant, the failure of the goods circulation to keep pace with population would actually have *raised* the price level. Instead of this being the fact, however, the price level actually fell. The fall therefore must have been due entirely to money scarcity per capita, and not in the least to any abundance of goods per capita.

(5) *Inflation,* 1896–1914. New gold mines were opened. The cyanide process for increasing gold production was introduced. Gold poured

from Colorado, Alaska, Canada and South Africa.

(6) *Further Inflation,* 1914–1917. Europe had paper money inflation and America would, of course, not accept paper money in payment for the munitions and food bought of us. Consequently the chief means of payment was gold; and there were large gold imports from Europe. There was also corresponding credit inflation, further promoted by the establishment of the Federal Reserve System. This new system made it legally possible to have a greater credit structure with the same gold base, or reserve.

(7) *Further Inflation,* 1917–1918. After America entered the War there was further gold inflation and credit inflation, for the same reasons as under "(6)." The credit inflation went on even more rapidly because the public, to lend to the government, borrowed the money from banks. This money, or credit currency, was not money already in existence, but was newly created by the banks simply writing it on their books. I remember once, when taking part in a speaking tour to help raise money for Liberty Loans, that a fellow speaker, a clergyman not versed in economics, appealed to his audience

as follows: "Lend money to Uncle Sam! That is, Buy Liberty Bonds. If you haven't any money to buy bonds with, go to your bank and borrow it. If the bank asks for security, tell them you'll let it have the bonds you buy with the money they lend you. It's like perpetual motion."

Too many people followed such advice. It *was* like perpetual motion, unsound. Instead of saving to lend they borrowed to lend. That is they really did not lend at all. The banks might just as well have loaned directly to the government, and even they did not save to lend but merely wrote "deposits" on their books. The same sort of make-believe loans were common in all the countries concerned in the War. The "lenders" went through the motion of lending but they were really merely inflating,—increasing the money flow without correspondingly increasing the goods flow.

(8) *Further Inflation,* 1918–1920. After the War the Victory Loan was floated by the same methods; and, to keep interest low, the Treasury brought pressure to bear on the Federal Reserve System. The low interest stimulated further borrowing for business purposes and speculation.

(9) *Deflation,* 1920–1922. A tightening of

credit requirements ensued, as a reaction against the previous inflation.

(10) *Slight Change,* 1922–1928. New Federal Reserve policy "to accommodate business."

A FORGOTTEN SUPPLY AND DEMAND

People who imagine that money has little or nothing to do with the level of prices usually tell us that "supply and demand settle the price of everything." In a sense, this may be admitted; but supply of, and demand for, what? The general tendency is to think only of the demand and supply of wheat, corn, sugar, steel, and other goods; and to forget entirely the demand and supply of money. Since the demand and supply of money cannot change the price of money in terms of money itself, they will work out their effects on the prices of other things, just as, we have noted, would be the case if a dollar were a dozen eggs. The demand and supply of eggs would not change the price of eggs in terms of eggs, and therefore would work out their effects on the prices of other things for which the eggs were exchanged.

If we go back to original trading, or barter, we can see the point more clearly. Suppose we were trading wheat for hogs. If the price of wheat in terms of hogs went down, we certainly would not say that the fall was due, necessarily and wholly, to the demand and supply of wheat alone; we would see that it could just as well be due to the demand and supply of hogs.

Evidently the same must be true if wheat is exchanged for silver; there is the silver demand and supply, as well as the wheat demand and supply. The same must be true if wheat is exchanged for gold—whether gold bullion, gold coin, gold certificates—or for other money convertible into gold. If there is a great deal of gold, or its substitutes—money convertible into gold —it will take more gold to buy a bushel of wheat than when the reverse is true; the greater the flow of money, the higher is the price level, and the reverse.

Evidently we ought never to forget the demand and supply of gold and its substitutes, the other kinds of money. Gold and its substitutes, paper money and bank deposits, enter into practically every exchange today. The demand and supply of money must have their effect upon the price level of every transaction. We see that a large supply of wheat makes wheat cheap. We must see that a large supply of dollars makes the dollar cheap, and that this implies a higher level of prices.

INDIVIDUAL AND GENERAL PRICE MOVEMENTS

It is true that the greater part of the price change of any *individual* commodity, like wheat, is due to the supply and demand relating to that individual commodity. For instance, only a small part of the fall in the price of cotton in 1926, following the unprecedented bumper crop of that year, can be ascribed to an increase in the value of money itself, as reflected in the *general level* of prices. Wheat has often gone up and down over 50 per cent, while the change of the general level of prices was only one or two per cent.

In exactly the same way the general sea level may not change an inch during a violent storm, though thousands of individual waves, moving up and down several feet many times, travel a total up and down distance of many miles. Throughout the most violent storms the level of the sea is chiefly affected by the flow of the tides. In the vast economic sea, with prices bobbing up and down (like waves), there is usually only a small net average change. We must learn therefore to distinguish between the *individual* movements of prices (caused by the demand and supply of individual commodities), movements which correspond to the waves, and the *general* movements of prices (caused by the demand and supply of money), movements which correspond to the tides.

Or, to go back to our bread and butter, the average thickness of the butter (the general level of prices) does not have much to do with the thickness at individual spots on the bread (individual prices). The butter at any spot may be thick or thin whatever the total amount of butter; only, if we press it thin in some places, it must get thicker somewhere else.

The level of prices might better be called the scale of prices. Just as we may magnify or shrink the scale of a map or picture without changing its individual outlines, so we may inflate or deflate the scale of prices without disturbing individual price relations.

This distinction between the two concepts, "individual prices" and "scale of prices," was drawn clearly in Germany during the period of her money inflation by the device of a "multiplicator." By this a hotel guest translated the printed prices on his bill of fare. He found the price of his dinner listed as, say, "6 marks," and the price of his room as "9 marks"; but, before he paid his bill, these figures had to be multiplied by the "multiplicator." This was a factor, or index, representing the price level, or scale of prices, and varied from day to day, going up as the mark went down. It had nothing to do with the real price of the dinner, either in terms of labor or relatively to the price of the room. Whether the multiplicator was 100,000 or 1,000,000 made no difference to these relations, but only changed the dinner and room from 600,000 and 900,000 to 6,000,000 and 9,000,000. The multiplicator, or index, saved the trouble of too frequently reprinting the price lists. The real price paid was the product of the list price by the multiplicator.

This principle applies universally, in America as well as in Germany. Every price paid is the product of an ideal price multiplied by an index; that is, it is partly a matter of supply and demand affecting the individual price, and partly a matter of relative inflation or deflation affecting the price level.

HOW INFLATION AND DEFLATION WORK

Even when a person is convinced that inflation and deflation do actually explain the rising and falling of the great tides of prices, he finds it hard to "see how" they operate. It may help him to "see" if he will suppose himself suddenly to have plenty of money through a loan obtained at the bank. He would then be in a position to buy more freely. When he exercises this new power to buy, he evidently tends to raise prices. If enough others, millions of people perhaps, are doing the same thing at the same time, as they did during the War, prices will rise.

People borrow money in order to buy things with it. When they borrow money of a bank they leave it on deposit only long enough to draw checks against it. Those who receive these checks then deposit them, and in turn draw checks, and thus the deposit originally created by the loan goes on circulating, and tends, every time it is used, to bid up, or keep up, the prices of the things bought. On the other hand, when it is hard to get money because banks will not lend, or for any other reason, there is less power to bid for goods. Prices then fall, because people lack money with which to pay.

CAUSES BEHIND INFLATION OR DEFLATION

Usually inflation comes when governments are in financial straits, especially in war time, or after a war has crippled the government's financial powers. War has always been by far the greatest expander of paper money and credit, and therefore the cause of the greatest price upheavals in history.

Paper money and credit inflation lower indirectly the value of gold itself. Thus, as we have noticed, the World War brought gold inflation to America because, when Europe had inflated with paper, her gold came to us.

The depreciation of gold in terms of its buying power in relation to commodities, caused by this gold inflation in America and elsewhere in the World War, was far greater than had ever occurred before from any other cause. As we have seen, the American gold dollar sank in purchasing power from 100 pre-war cents in 1913 to 40 pre-war cents in 1920, or as much as our paper greenbacks depreciated during the Civil War period.

But not all inflation occurs in times of war; there may be very considerable inflation in times of peace. Even gold inflation may occur in times of peace, either from increased discoveries of gold, as from those already mentioned in California and Australia in the middle of the 19th Century, and from those in Colorado, Alaska,

Canada and South Africa, at the end of that century, or from certain improvements in metallurgy, such as the cyanide process of gold extraction.

Credit inflation, especially, may occur in times of peace, caused either by changes in banking laws or by changes in banking customs. For instance, the passage of the Federal Reserve Act, while praiseworthy in the extreme as an improvement on the inelastic National banking system, would have tended toward inflation, even if the War had never occurred, simply by reducing the legal requirements as to gold reserves, thus increasing greatly the possible expansion of credit.

Turning to deflation, this may be caused by the exhaustion of gold mines; by government action in reducing the volume of money in circulation; or by the action of banks in restricting credit.

Deflation of paper money has most frequently been brought about by the effort to resume gold redemption after a war. This was the case in the United States between 1865 and 1879, and in England after the World War in 1918. Italy started on the same project in 1926, but has since wisely abandoned it.

SUMMARY

In summary, we may say that there are three great disturbers of monetary standards: Governmental policies—especially but not exclusively in war time; banking policies usually linked with the Governmental; and fluctuations in gold production.

War, generally speaking, makes for the greatest inflation, while the greatest deflation is brought about *after* war, if a government tries to get back to the pre-war gold standard.

It is important to note that, in either case, whether of inflation or deflation, the causes lie in human policies which, for the most part, certainly in peace time, could be modified so as to prevent inflation or deflation if leaders and people understood clearly the nature and function of money and the effects of inflation and deflation.

The chief conclusions of this chapter are two:

(1) The general level of prices is raised or lowered (that is the purchasing power of money is lowered or raised) by *relative* inflation or deflation—by the circulation of money outrunning that of goods, or the reverse.

(2) In actual fact the money flow is so un-

steady as compared with the goods flow that, in practically all important cases, the inflation or deflation is not only relative but also absolute; there is an absolute increase or decrease in the per capita money flow without any great change in the per capita goods flow.

We can, therefore, usually omit the qualifying adjectives "relative" and "absolute" and say simply: The dollar usually falls through inflation, and rises through deflation.

CHAPTER IV

THE DIRECT HARM FROM INFLATION AND DEFLATION

MONEY MORE VARIABLE THAN GOODS

AS stated in the last chapter, the public imagine that a low price level is due to an abundance of goods and a "high cost of living" to a scarcity of goods—that a fall or rise of the price level represents a sort of feast or famine in goods. We have found, on the contrary, that it represents, rather, a famine or feast in money. The inflation and deflation are not merely relative; they are usually also absolute.

Once this important fact is recognized, the whole aspect of rising and falling price levels will change in the public mind. A "high cost of living" in which there was a real scarcity of food, clothing, shelter, and other goods, would mean a general impoverishment, a lowering of per capita real income; but a "high cost of living" caused by inflation does not—not directly, at least—mean any *average* reduction in human wellbeing; or it does not, to put it another way, mean any lessening of the stream of goods per capita.

Evidently, if a man who formerly got $2,000 a year now gets $4,000, while the prices of all things he has to buy are also exactly doubled, he is no worse off and no better off than before. His present-day dollar buys only half of what his former dollar bought; but, as he has two dollars for every one he had before, his real condition has not changed.

The high cost of living, which alarmed many people before and during the World War, was actually accompanied by a corresponding higher average of money incomes, and therefore did not mean, as those people imagined, any great progressive impoverishment of the nation. Nor did the depression of 1921 mean, as was then (and still is) commonly thought, that there was an over-abundance of products (a surplus of the stream of goods).

Even in Germany when prices rose many billions of times, money incomes also rose many billions, though not *as* many billions, of times. If money incomes had remained the same as before the War even a hundred fold rise of the level of prices would be unendurable; it would have meant starvation and death for almost all Germans. The actual conditions were not as bad as that.

"MERELY" A BOOKKEEPING CHANGE

But if we grant that price movements are chiefly movements in the value of money, the question naturally arises: What of it? The money yardstick changes, but the thing measured does not greatly change. What harm can there be if prices double simply because money is plentiful and not because goods are scarce? We use twice as many dollars to buy things with simply because we have twice as many dollars to use. Is this not merely, or chiefly, a matter of bookkeeping? How, then, can it be of any real importance?

It would, indeed, be of no importance if everybody's income were adjusted to the change in prices. But this is not and cannot be the case. Even if our physical yardstick should vary, such a change, though purely a bookkeeping matter, would confuse all commitments of merchants made in terms of yards, such as sales of cloth, carpet or wire. This would be serious; but a change in the money yardstick, the dollar, is far more serious, and for three reasons:

(1) The physical yardstick merely affects the sales of those few goods which happen to be measured in yards. It is important in the ribbon market but not in the wheat, sugar, cotton, coal, oil, lumber, or steel markets. Its variations would not affect the sales of goods measured in bushels, quarts, cords, pounds, tons, acres, gallons, kilowatts, or days' work.

The monetary yardstick, on the other hand, affects all sales. In every sale where we find the yard as the goods-unit, we find the dollar as the money-unit; so many *yards* of carpet are sold for so many *dollars* of money. Likewise every commitment in pounds, bushels, quarts or anything else, involves a commitment in dollars. The dollar is used as much as all other units put together.

If, then, we are at such pains to standardize or stabilize the yard, the pound, and every other goods-unit, having—as we do—official sealers of weights and measures to prevent the cheating of the public because of changes in those goods-units, how much more important is it to stabilize the unit of money, applying, as it does, to every purchase and sale!

(2) This monetary yardstick is used for long-time contracts, in which the dollars of to-day are exchanged for dollars of the future. There are, to be sure, time contracts in yards and other units, but they are far less frequent, less important and of shorter duration. They generally imply money also, as when future wheat is sold. Practically never do we exchange present yards of cloth for future yards, present tons of coal for future tons. But we are constantly contracting to pay present dollars for future dollars. If a man contracts to pay you a certain number of dollars, ten years hence, for a loan of a certain number of dollars today, it makes a tremendous difference both to him and to you whether the dollars in which you are paid have meanwhile shrunk or expanded. It makes a tremendous difference, for instance, to a bond holder.

This evil (Number 2) is far more serious than the first (Number 1). The great network of long-time contracts, running months, years, generations, or even centuries, includes hundreds of billions of dollars in promises to pay money

—promissory notes, mortgages, debentures, railway bonds, government bonds, leases, annuities, pensions, insurance policies, savings bank deposits, and so on.

(3) A change in the physical yardstick would be at once detected. But the disastrous effects of the subtle change in the dollar are not perceived because of the Money Illusion. Added havoc is thus wrought because the source of the trouble is unrecognized. If we knew how our dollar changed, we could, to a certain extent, provide against it, just as we can largely provide against the harm done by one other variable unit still in use, the month. We know in advance that February is a short month and March a long one.

For these three reasons, then—the universality of the use of the monetary unit in exchange; its unique use in time contracts; and the invisibility of its tricks—our unstable dollar is vastly more harmful than an unstable physical yardstick or pound weight would be.

INJUSTICE BETWEEN DEBTOR AND CREDITOR

Think of the disturbance of loan contracts. When, for instance, there is inflation, and the price level rises, the creditors lose and the debtors gain.

It might seem at first that this is as broad as it is long since the debtor gains exactly as much as the creditor loses. It might be argued that no harm can be done to society as a whole either by inflation or deflation since the average wealth would not be changed.

But one might as well reason that when a bank vault is robbed or when your house is burglarized, society is none the poorer. If you, the victim of the robbery, should be told, "What you have lost the burglar has gained, and therefore society as a whole is just as well off!" that would be cold comfort to you.

In somewhat the same sense this burglarizing dollar is defrauding people, even if it does so impersonally. Something is taken away from its rightful owner. The evil is not (primarily at least) general impoverishment; it is social injustice. Unlike burglary or personal fraud, there is no violation of the letter of the law as to debts, but there is a defeat of its spirit and intent.

EUROPEAN EXAMPLES

Extreme examples are always the clearest. The story is told of a Polish clothier, deciding to retire from business, who sold his 100 suits of clothes for 100,000 Polish marks and invested the proceeds in a "secure" three-year mortgage at 6 per cent, thus receiving 18,000 Polish marks in interest and the safe return of his 100,000 Polish marks of principal at the end of three years. But this whole 118,000 Polish marks would then buy only one suit of clothes! Nominally he had received 6% interest. Actually he had lost practically all, interest and principal alike.

A famous professor at Berlin had made a small fortune from the sale of his books. He invested it in so-called "safe" bonds with the expectation of living on the income. At the end of the inflation period he found that his whole fortune, the accumulation of a life-time of hard work, would not buy a postage stamp! Yet the bonds were not defaulted. He was ruined, not because the promise to pay was not fulfilled, not because goods became scarce and therefore dear, not because his judgment was bad; but because inflation depreciated the mark in buying power almost to zero.

In the city of Budapest a benevolent woman founded a genteel poorhouse for just such victims of inflation. When a friend of mine visited that poorhouse he was shown into a little hall bedroom, with one small iron bedstead for two people, a dry-goods box for a washstand and on that a tin wash basin. There, he was told, lived two judges of the highest court who had invested their savings in bonds and other "safe" securities. Currency depreciation had reduced the buying power of their once ample incomes to practically nothing. They had become objects of charity.

One of the German witnesses who appeared before the Dawes' Commission was a workingman, representing, he said, fifteen million German laborers. When asked what labor most needed, he said, "a more stable currency." He said the workmen had no way to lay up for a rainy day, to put by money in order to have it ready to pay the doctor and nurse at the coming of a baby into the family, or to provide for old age or funeral expenses. The mark would lose much of its buying power over night. A wife would meet her husband when he got his wages, snatch the money and run to the grocer to spend it before the soaring prices should soar still higher.

Millions of European savings bank depositors had their life savings .swept away. Because of the Money Illusion, few had the understanding to withdraw their deposits in the early stages of inflation, and, had they done so, still fewer would have known how to reinvest them wisely so as to profit by the price movements.

In many countries of Europe the inflation during and after the World War literally ruined millions of middle class investors who had invested in bonds; they were the creditors and lost practically their whole principal by the fall of the German mark, the Polish mark, the Russian ruble, and the Austrian crown. These investors—including teachers, lawyers, judges, clergymen, physicians, clerks, depositors in savings banks, the small holders of bonds, the recipients of life insurance money—have now come to be called "the new poor of Europe." Some of these, who had every reason to expect to retire in comfort, are now day laborers, doing anything at all to scrape together a bare subsistence in their old age.

In Austria a striking example was found by another economist, Professor James Harvey Rogers. A bank, as is not unusual in that country, had possession of a number of paper mills. Not wishing to be called a "profiteer," this bank adopted a mechanical system of charging. Beginning with the raw material, the wood pulp, which was paid for in Austrian crowns, the manager added a fixed ten per cent for one expense, then fifteen per cent for another, and so on, thus building up a cost structure until a "fair price" was worked out for the finished product. According to their books these mills were making profits.

One day one of the mills burned down and the manager was forced to sell the stock of wood pulp on hand before it had been manufactured into paper. Between the time when he had bought that wood pulp and placed it on inventory at cost price, and the time of sale, after the burning of the mill, there had been such a depreciation of the crown that the price of wood pulp, along with everything else, had "gone up" enormously. Accordingly, when the wood pulp was sold, it was found that, by the books, the mill which had burned down had made larger profits than any of those which had remained in operation! The truth was simply that they had lost all around, but that the loss was less on the unmanufactured pulp than on the manufactured paper. They had failed to translate their accounts into buying power; they had reckoned in terms of the crown as if it were fixed and stable, whereas it was unfixed and unstable.

Yet, strangely enough, while inflation is going on, the general public finds it hard to admit that there can be too much money. Money, however abundant, always seems scarce.

After a rapid inflation once starts, the clamor for more money often grows louder and louder.

The most striking example of the Money Illusion in relation to inflation may be found in Germany. The President of the Reichsbank, speaking before the Reichstag on August 7, 1923, flatly stated, "the note-issue at present amounts to 63,000,000,000,000,000; in a few days we shall be able to issue in one day two-thirds of the total circulation." The strangest thing was the matter of course way in which this casual announcement was received. Here was inflation going on at terrific speed and ever accelerating, yet no one seemed to care how it would inevitably end.

This heedless optimism reminds one of the definition of an optimist, suggested by a famous Yale wit (William Lyon Phelps), as a man who, having fallen out of a nineteenth story window, was heard to mutter just before striking the ground "so far so good."

A few, of course, grow rich during inflation by going into debt and then having their debts virtually wiped out by that inflation. Hugo Stinnes, the famous war-time millionaire of Germany, was an outstanding example. Sometimes the same people or families who profited by inflation got caught in the reverse tide of deflation, and were ruined. The Stinnes heirs were examples.

AMERICAN EXAMPLES

Even America has not escaped these evils. A workingman who, in 1896, had put one hundred dollars into a savings bank found, in 1920, that his principal, plus compound interest at 4½ per cent, amounted to about three hundred dollars. On the face of it he had his principal back and in addition $200 of profit, or accumulated interest. This $200 seemed a genuine reward of thrift. But it was an illusory profit like the "profit" on the shirt sold by the woman in Germany, mentioned in the first chapter, or the "profit" of the paper mills in Austria, just mentioned. The appearance of profit was due to a sort of bogus accounting in terms of a varying dollar.

When our American depositor came to spend his $300 in 1920 he found prices nearly four times as high as they had been in 1896; consequently his entire accumulation of $300 would buy only about three-quarters as much as his original $100 would buy in 1896. He would have come off better if he had spent his hundred dollars in 1896. If he had turned his $100 into furniture, jewelry or some other representative commodity in 1896 and simply held that commodity until 1920, he would have had the use and benefit of it during all that period, together with a big advantage over the man who saved; for this commodity would have "appreciated" about four fold. As it was, his only reward of thrift was punishment. He had really lost, not only his interest, but also part of his principal.

It can all be put in figures. He deposited 100 dollars in 1896. In 1920, each of these dollars was worth 26⅔ cents of the 1896 buying standard. He took out 300 dollars in 1920, worth $300 \times .26\frac{2}{3} = 80$ dollars of the 1896 standard. In short, he put in 100 dollars and took out the equivalent of 80 such dollars. Instead of having, as interest, something over and above his $100 of principal he had really lost 20 dollars of his original principal. Instead of receiving a reward for his self-denial, the saver was heavily mulcted for his abstinence and forethought by our will-o'-the-wisp dollar. There was really no such thing as interest. It was all wiped out by the fall of the dollar. If the reader is astonished and incredulous to learn that our magic dollar made interest vanish, it is because the Money Illusion has hitherto hid the truth from him.

Chart IV shows in graphic form the apparent gain in 1920 dollars of the depositor and his real loss as measured in 1896 dollars. The loss of twenty 1896 dollars was equal in buying power to a loss of seventy-five dollars of 1920.

Before 1896, Hetty Green and Russell Sage had made fortunes by loaning at low rates of interest. Had they tried this during the period between 1896 and 1920 they would have had their labor for their pains, much worry and no profit. At the end of that time they would have been poorer than at the beginning.

Suppose Sage had started with a million dollars in 1896, investing it at 4½ per cent interest, reinvesting year after year; he would have been in exactly the same situation as the savings bank depositor, only on a larger scale. He would have had $3,000,000 in 1920 dollars; but this would be equivalent only to $800,000 in 1896 dollars. In that period all thrift or saving, by rich and poor alike, was not rewarded but penalized.

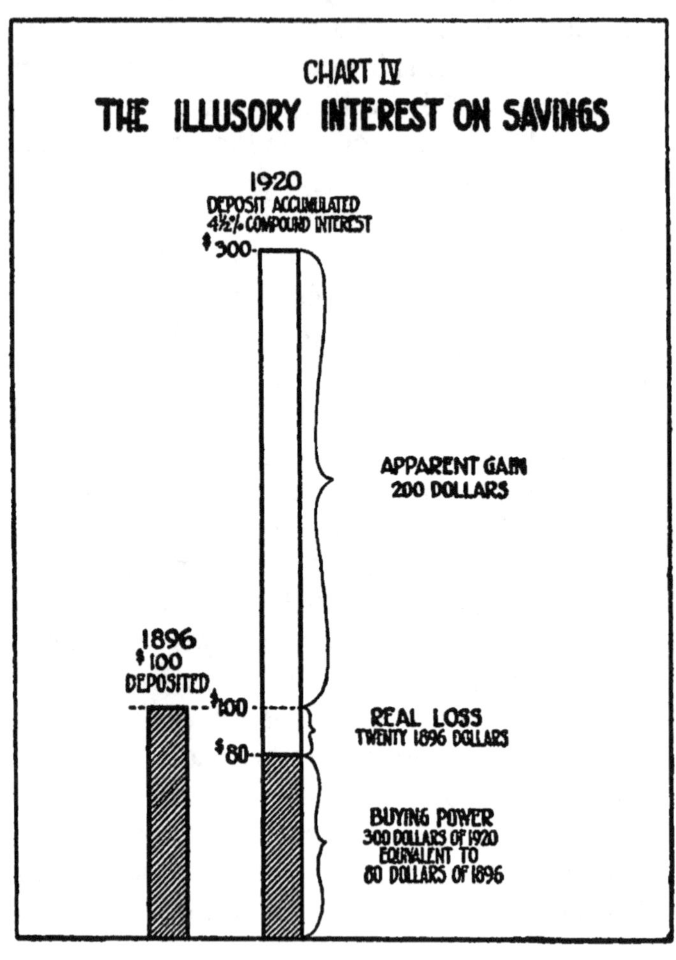
CHART IV
THE ILLUSORY INTEREST ON SAVINGS
1920
DEPOSIT ACCUMULATED
4½% COMPOUND INTEREST
$300
APPARENT GAIN
200 DOLLARS
1896
$100
DEPOSITED
$100
REAL LOSS
TWENTY 1896 DOLLARS
$80
BUYING POWER
300 DOLLARS OF 1920
EQUIVALENT TO
80 DOLLARS OF 1896

AMERICAN BONDS AND MORTGAGES

Any gold bond bought in 1896 and running to 1920, or any intermediate date, proved to be a veritable gold brick. Yet, because of the Money Illusion, even to this day few know it. Yale University lost heavily during the no-interest period. Yale had recently to ask for a further endowment of $20,000,000, largely, as President Angell said, because of the fall in the purchasing power of the dollar. About $7,000,000 of the new endowment was required to restore the purchasing power of the income from the bonds, mortgages and notes held in 1914. Of course, the same sort of losses were sustained by other endowed universities, foundations, hospitals and churches.

A business man who prided himself on his "safe" investments and who was the manager of a $30,000,000 estate recently boasted that in all the years of his management he had never lost a cent. A young man, just then beginning his work as "investment counsel" succeeded in convincing him that, on the contrary, by his policy of investing only in bonds and mortgages he had really lost two-thirds of the estate's original value, because the dollar had shrunk that much during the period of his investment.

And yet this shrinkage of principal was overlooked while this cautious manager haggled over some fractional advantage in the interest on his supposedly safe investments. John E. Rovensky, First Vice-President of the Bank of America, put it well: "What a mockery it is for bankers to debate for days as to whether a twenty-year bond shall be sold to the public on a 4.75 per cent or 4.78 per cent interest basis when it is uncertain as to whether the principal amount of the bond will be repaid on an 80 per cent, 100 per cent or 120 per cent basis! We dedicate tomes of deep study to the question of whether the tendency of interest rates during the next ten years will be up or down one or two per cent, and, at the same time, we leave to chance and to haphazard measures whether the value of the principal will go up or down ten or twenty per cent. Fortunately the business men and bankers of the country are beginning to realize the situation and are ready to support a movement toward a study of the evil and its remedies."

REAL INTEREST AND MONEY INTEREST

Just as the Money Illusion hides the distinction between money wages and real wages, so it hides a distinction between money interest and real interest. The rate of interest in terms of money and the rate of interest in terms of commodities are not the same unless we have a stable price level. If the price level rises 1 per cent per annum, a 5 per cent rate of interest in terms of money is really a 4 per cent rate in terms of what money buys. If prices are falling 1 per cent, the nominal 5 per cent is really 6 per cent.

During the period 1896 to 1920 the real rate of interest was wiped out, as we have seen. It was less than nothing. But in 1921 in a period of deflation real interest rose as high as 60 per cent. That is, in brief, why a certain well-known American millionaire, who was caught in debt, lost nearly his whole fortune of $150,000,000.

THE AMERICAN FARMER

In this same period the farmer suffered and, as we all know, his sufferings are not yet over. Our tricky dollar had turned the tables on him completely. During the period of inflation and rapidly rising price level our farmers, lured by the hope of large profits and urged by patriotic pleas to win the war with wheat, corn, hogs, and beef, increased the acreage and the yield of farm crops far beyond the peace-time normal. Many farmers were induced to buy land at prices proportionate to the temporarily swollen profits. All this overstimulation of production was bad; the overstimulation of speculation in land values was still worse. But these evils could have been met and overcome without disastrous consequences had the inflated prices been left approximately at the mountain high level of 1920.

But *deflation* followed. Farmers who had extended cultivation on the basis of $2.50 wheat now found they were unable to sell even at $1.00 per bushel, although one-half the world was hungry for wheat and perhaps one-tenth of the whole population was suffering from famine. Those farmers who through the urge of patriotism or profits had purchased farm lands at top-notch prices were unable to meet their notes. They lost, not only the land they had recklessly purchased "on margin" but all the payments they had made thereon.

But this is only the beginning of the story. Thousands of banks took over scores of thousands of farms, not because they wanted them, but because they were all the banks could get upon the loans advanced to farmers. Hundreds of these banks failed and bank failures, in turn, caused failures of manufacturing or merchandising establishments.

"SAFE" INVESTMENTS BY TRUSTEES

Widows and orphans are the special victims of "safe" investments. A lady was left a legacy of $50,000 by her father in 1892 about the time that the dollar was worth the most. The money was put in trust and was invested in so-called "safe" bonds. In 1920, when the dollar was worth the least, I accompanied her on a visit to the trustee. The trustee began to explain how careful he had been about the investment of this money. He told her that he still had the principal intact, with the exception of $2,000, the loss of which, he explained at length, was not his fault but came about because of an unwise investment made by her father in some railway bonds.

Observing my amusement, he inquired the reason. I replied: "You say that there has been a loss of $2,000 out of the $50,000 or only four per cent; but actually there has been a loss of about seventy-five per cent."

He said: "What do you mean? You can look at my books."

Of course, I did not doubt his honesty. I explained to him that the $50,000 which had been put in his hands on behalf of the lady was the equivalent of about $190,000 in 1920. I added: "You haven't the $190,000; you just said that you have only $48,000. There is a loss of nearly 75 per cent. Moreover, you have been paying this lady $2,500 or $3,000 a year. She has been living on it. You and she called it income, and you both thought she was getting interest; but, as a matter of fact, she has merely been eating up her principal all the time. To have kept up her principal in buying power you should have reinvested each year enough income to act as a sinking fund against the depreciation of the principal. But there was not enough income for that. Even if you had reinvested all you paid her you would not now have the $190,000 required. Furthermore, that $2,500 or $3,000 a year which you paid her is worth only a quarter as much now as when you began to send it to her. Just as this lady's income and principal was only one quarter (in value) of what it was when this trust began, so every bondholder's 'steady' income is a delusion and a snare, so long as we have an unsteady dollar. Your books are all wrong because you are using a wrong unit which plays tricks on you and this lady, even mixing up interest and principal. The dollar is just as truly a false or variable unit as is the mark; $50,000 today is no more truly the same as $50,000 of 1892 than 50,000 marks today are the same as 50,000 marks of 1892."

He finally acknowledged this, but insisted: "It wasn't my fault."

"It is not your fault individually," I remarked, "but you men who are taking care of property of widows and orphans have a public obligation to take an interest in these great problems which are everybody's business in general and therefore nobody's business in particular."

"But," he replied, "everybody loses, doesn't he, from the high cost of living?"

"No," I said, "others have won what this lady lost. It wasn't their fault that, in this great gamble, they won at her expense any more than it is your fault; it is the fault of the unstable dollar. But this means it is the fault of all of us for not correcting that fluctuating measure of value."

He inquired: "Who has won what she has lost?"

I answered: "She is a creditor—a bondholder. The debtors—the stockholders—won it."

"WHO GOT THE MONEY?"

To illustrate how, as between stockholders and bondholders, this lottery works, consider a company which, say, before the War in 1913 had outstanding a hundred million dollars of bonded debt and a hundred million dollars of stock. Each yields five per cent, five million dollars, so that, before the War, the corporation distributed between these two classes of investors, bondholders and stockholders, ten million dollars. This, for convenience, will be called profit. Let us now see what happens if the buying power of the dollar is cut in two, that is, if the price level doubles (which it actually did between 1913 and 1919). Suppose then, that this company did the same physical volume of business after the War as it did before, but at the doubled price level. It would then have doubled the profit—in dollars. For, if the expenses double and the receipts double, the difference between the two must also double. The profit would thus be twenty million dollars instead of ten million dollars. But while nominally this twenty million of profit would be double the original ten million, in real value it of course would merely be its equivalent.

Now this twenty million dollars would not be distributed evenly between bondholders and stockholders, as the ten million had been! Why? Because the bondholders are restricted by contract to their five per cent. They will get, out of the twenty million, the same five million as before—the same, that is, nominally, but in real value only half. What is left out of the twenty million (fifteen million dollars) will now go to the stockholders. Nominally, then, the stockholders will get three times what they did before the War, but when we allow for the dollar having been depreciated one-half, what they really get is one and one-half times as much value.

Thus the stockholders get more real value than before the War, while the bondholders get correspondingly less. Inflation, quite impersonally, if you please, has picked the pockets of the bondholders and put the value into the stockholders' pockets, simply by the change in the value of the dollar.

Suppose, now, that the wind blows the other way. Then the exact opposite happens. Prices are, let us say, cut in two by deflation and the company's expenses and receipts are both cut in two. It follows that the profits will also be halved. Hence the company will distribute not $10,000,000 but $5,000,000. (Of course, the $5,000,000, at this lower price level, is worth just as much as the $10,000,000 before.) But this $5,000,000 will not be evenly divided between stockholders and bondholders; for, under their contracts, the bondholders are entitled to five per cent. They will therefore take the entire $5,000,000, leaving nothing at all for the stockholders. The company is on the verge of bankruptcy. If the process goes much further a receivership follows. The blame would be attributed to the management; but it would be the robber dollar that had done the harm.

Like the stockholder is the farmer, already discussed, who mortgaged his farm, while his creditor is like the bondholder. When, as in 1919, there is inflation, the farmer gains at the expense of his creditor. When, as in 1921, there is deflation, his creditor gains at the expense of the farmer.

THE WAR DEBTS

Governments lose and gain in the same great gamble. The effects of inflation and deflation on the huge war debts are interesting. In a Memorandum on Public Finance, 1922–1926, of the League of Nations, the public debts of the countries of the world are recalculated to give their equivalent in pre-war buying power. We find that Italy in 1914 owed 16 billion lire but in 1925 owed the equivalent of only 13 billion (of pre-war buying power). That is, in spite of the huge war expenses which enormously increased the debt in lire, the real debt burden had actually decreased because of the depreciation of the lira. What the debtor Italian government gained by this inflation, its creditors (Italian and foreign citizens) lost.

The depreciation of the German mark, of course, practically wiped out Germany's internal debt, although after the paper mark disappeared Germany had the grace to "revalorize" her domestic debt; that is, she has undertaken to repay it in part so that she still owes on that account the equivalent of one and three-fourths billion gold marks. Individual Germans and German companies were not always so gracious. One large steamship company is said to have paid off its entire bonded debt, originally a huge one, running into many millions of dollars, for the equivalent of $1100.

(The only countries in the War whose internal war debts have not thus been largely cancelled by inflation seem to be the United States, Great Britain, and the self-governing Dominions of the British Empire. Canada's real debt burden was multiplied by the War more than four and one-half fold; Great Britain's, six and one-half fold; America's, eleven fold; Australia's, fourteen fold.)

We must not infer, however, that the cost of the War to the public was lessened by inflation. What the taxpayers gained through depreciation of the currency was taken from them again as lenders and savers. The burden of the public debt was not lightened; it was only shifted from the shoulders of the taxpayers to the shoulders of the investors.

But this injustice as to public debts was as nothing compared with the injustice as to private debts. The great mass of private lenders were of course obliged to accept depreciated money in payment for their loans.

An insurance contract is like a bond; for it is an agreement to pay a certain sum at a future date, but implies nothing about the buying power of the sum to be paid. European inflation defrauded widows of most of the insurance for which their husbands had paid. Even in the United States, a widow receiving $10,000 insurance at her husband's death in 1920, which had been contracted for in 1896, was, of course, getting only one quarter of the value contracted for.

SALARIES AND WAGES

Salaries and wage contracts are also like bonds. Although they run for shorter periods and may be readjusted, they seldom are readjusted promptly or fully. When prices are rising, wages and salaries are, as it were, running after a lost train. The dean of a Western college writes me that he began his work in 1914 at a salary of $2,800. He might naturally have expected by 1925, after eleven years of service, to have received a substantial increase. The fact was, however, that his salary then was $5,000. Although, on the face of it, this $5,000 was nearly double his 1914 salary, we find, if we translate it into 1914 dollars, that it is worth about $3,000, or only a little more than the original $2,800.

THE EXTENT OF THIS SOCIAL INJUSTICE

The extent of this subtle impersonal robbing, or transfer of values from creditors to debtors through inflation or the reverse through deflation, is enormous. Professor Willford I. King, of the National Bureau of Economic Research, one of the best American statisticians, estimated that, in the United States alone, where the evil of unstable money had been incomparably less than in many other countries, there has been this sort of picking of the pockets of one set of people for the advantage of another to the tune of sixty billions of dollars, and this within a period of only half a dozen years (1914–1920). All of this robbery was legal though contrary to the principles of essential right as laid down by the Constitution of the United States and the courts of the land; it was property taken without due process of law.

Suppose there should be a sixty *million* dollar bank robbery; an account of it would be on the front page of every newspaper. Yet this sixty *billion* "robbery" by inflation—one thousand times as great—was so subtly accomplished that it was not generally recognized when it happened and is not recognized now. Were it not for the Money Illusion, the losses and gains of these prodigious sums would be known and the reasons for them clearly understood. A legislative bill of complaint would be filed by persons whose property had been confiscated, restitution demanded and the mischievous dollar corrected, or else there would be protests, riots and rebellion.

GAMBLING IN GOLD MINES

As things now are every contract in a gold standard country is a gamble in the future value of the gold dollar. If new gold fields are developed, or new metallurgical processes are developed, or a new banking system is introduced economizing gold, that metal is likely to fall in value. If gold production falls off it is pretty sure to rise. Contracts in gold dollars are unconscious wagers on which of these two things will happen.

As we have seen there can be no such thing as a safe bond or other promise to be paid dollars until we have a safe dollar. What does the promise to be paid one thousand "dollars" fifty years from now amount to? It is the promise to be paid one thousand X's,—unknown quantities. We are very careful to hedge around the promise—by guarantees, liens, mortgages—so that those one thousand X's will surely be paid; but we are not at all careful as to what the X is—simply because it is carelessly assumed, taken for granted, that it will remain the same. We think we have made a loan "secure," and talk of "securities" without realizing what mockeries such terms are.

The chief indictment, then, of our present dollar is that it is uncertain in value. As long as it is used as a measuring stick, every contract is necessarily a lottery, and every contracting party is compelled to be a gambler in gold without his own consent.

The very people, those buying only "gilt edged" gold bonds, who would be afraid to invest in gold mining enterprises, stake their whole fortunes on the fitful value of the products of those mines. They are often the biggest gamblers in the world but do not know it. During the last generation they have lost in this gamble more than all the gamblers, strictly so called, in the world, and yet do not know it.

There are now at stake hundreds of billions of dollars' worth of bonds in gold standard countries, the holders of which are in blissful ignorance of the existence of any such risk.

The business man is likewise gambling in gold in addition to assuming the risks of his own business. Business is always injured by uncertainty. Uncertainty paralyzes effort, and uncertainty in the purchasing power of the dollar is the worst of all business uncertainties.

It will do no good, of course, to rail at the lucky winners in the lottery. The public was greatly mistaken in attributing low prices to the "strangle-hold" of wicked bondholders, and is equally mistaken in attributing high prices to the personal turpitude of profiteers. The fault is not theirs. While they have, in a sense, won their neighbors' stakes or picked their neighbors' pockets, they did so without intent to defraud. They are like the rest of the general public, unconscious gamblers. They have simply played the game. We should stop the game, not blame the winners.

One of the chief signs of a high civilization is the reduction of risks and the lessening of the many perils of life and property to which human beings are exposed. We therefore introduce elaborate plans of insurance. We start "safety first" campaigns. We fix and safeguard all weights and measures, except the most important. Judged by this safety criterion our unstable dollar is a relic of barbarism.

CHAPTER V

THE INDIRECT HARM FROM INFLATION AND DEFLATION

UNSTABLE MONEY—UNSTABLE BUSINESS

WE have now seen that the unstable dollar upsets contracts and financial arrangements of many kinds and thus produces grave social injustice amounting to a subtle sort of pocket picking on a giant scale.

But this "pocket picking" is only the first effect. Other, and more indirect, effects follow. First of all, unstable money explains at least part of the secret of business fluctuations, the so-called "business cycles"! Booms, recessions, liquidation and recovery have long puzzled the business world. While certain plausible, and partially true, explanations have readily been given, they were as incomplete and unconvincing as the German shop woman's explanations (quoted in the first chapter) of the "high cost of living" and its effect upon the price of the shirt, and for the same reason. Wherever unstable money does its work we find the public mystified; for unstable money remains behind the scenes. Its tricks are like those of a sleight-of-hand artist. Because of the Money Illusion, one of the principal causes of booms and panics is unperceived. Only after an economic and statistical analysis do we come to realize that trade fluctuations are caused, in large part, by *changes* in the buying power of the dollar.

Monetary depreciation (rising price level) stimulates, and monetary appreciation (falling price level) depresses business. The reason is simple. When producers get higher prices they do not, at first, have to pay correspondingly higher costs; for instance, wages and salaries do not rise so fast, being fixed by contract for months or years in advance. Much less do they, at first, have to pay higher rent and interest. Such lagging of important expenses usually involves a lagging of total expenses behind total receipts. Consequently, profits, the excess of receipts over expenses, tend at first to increase. Conversely, a falling price level diminishes profits.

Now the profit-taker is the captain of industry on whose decision depends the rate of output. Hence it follows that, when the price level rises and profits increase, industry is expanded and business booms; but when profits decrease, industry is contracted and business is depressed.

The profit-taker thus follows the profit motive, but, even while doing so, he is likely to be misled by the Money Illusion. For instance, during inflation the cost of raw materials and other costs seem to be lower than they really are. When the costs were incurred the dollar was worth more than it is later when the product is sold, so that the dollars in the original cost and the dollars in the later sale are not the same dollars. The manufacturer is deceived just as was the German shopkeeper or the Austrian paper manufacturers who thought they were making profits. Many a manufacturer has been lured by such *apparently* high profits into expanding his output and extending himself in debt, only to find, as soon as the tide turned, that he was ruined by his over-expansion.

This is simply one more example of the confusion created by an ever-changing dollar and the consequent falsification of a business man's accounts. In general, the effect of the unstable dollar is to expand business unduly during inflation and to contract it unduly during deflation. Thus business staggers as the dollar staggers.

One of my own statistical studies shows that almost every fall in the buying power of the dollar leads a little later to an increase in the volume of trade; while almost every rise in the dollar leads to a decrease in that volume. The statistics of bankruptcies and unemployment follow this same relation to the changes in the dollar. Chart V shows the relationship between *changes* in the price level and the volume of trade.

UNSTABLE MONEY—UNSTABLE EMPLOYMENT

Few economic problems have seemed more baffling than the unemployment problem, although none is of greater human interest or has received more attention. This relation of unstable employment to unstable money has been studied extensively by the International Labour Office at Geneva from its establishment in 1920. M. Henri Fuss, Chief of the Unemployment Service of the Office, has shown that, during the period 1919–25, deflation occurred in 22 countries and was followed by a depression of trade and increased unemployment in all these countries, with three unimportant exceptions.

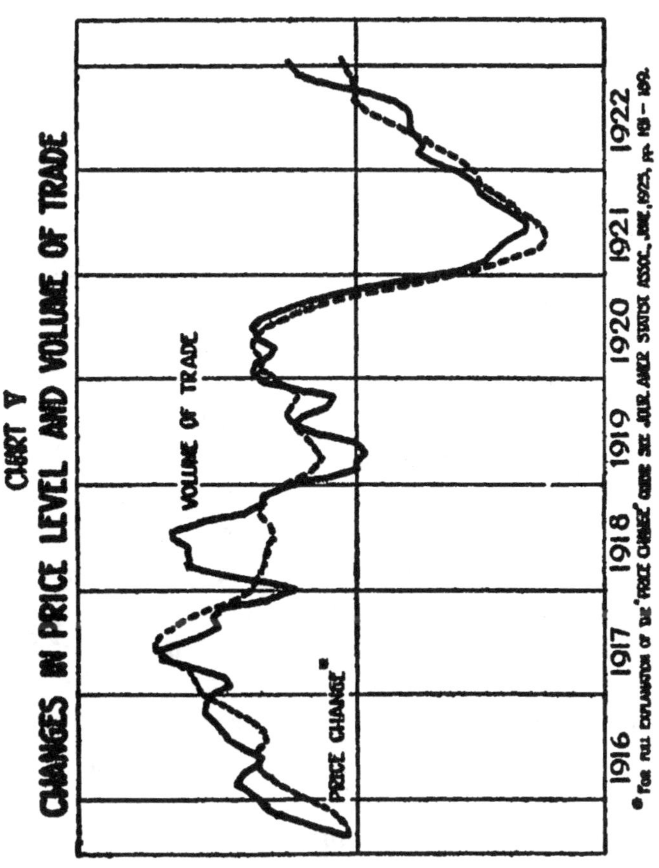

In the United States and England, the deflation of 1920–21 threw millions out of work. Unemployment became the mother of revolutionary unrest. In England a second deflation was brought about in 1925–26 in order to bring the British pound back to the gold basis, at the old ratio of $4.86⅝ to the pound sterling. Again came unemployment, labor discontent, and with this condition the greatest strike in England's history. The British Home Secretary estimated the cost of the strike at two billions of dollars—"a loss greater even than that of the South African War." Of course, other causes were involved in the loss; but deflation was a powerful factor, and all the greater because hidden from view by the Money Illusion.

This second English deflation tended to drag down the American price level also and this American deflation is, I think, one cause for American unemployment today.

In Poland a different policy from England's was pursued. There had been inflation after the War, playing havoc with exchange rates, wages and taxes. During the two years' inflation following June, 1924, Poland's price level had risen from an equilibrium with the price levels of the gold standard world to a level more than 50 per cent higher. Price increases were adjusted to the new level. The Kemmerer Commission, therefore, justly deemed it "economically unwise and politically impracticable" to try to bring the zloty back to its original par with the gold franc. Instead they advised stabilizing it where it was. In this way the unemployment and depression which had followed the policy of deflation in England were avoided.

THE INTERESTS OF LABOR

The interests of labor, especially, lie in the stabilization of the monetary unit. The laborer is the victim not only of unemployment caused by deflation but also of the high cost of living caused by inflation. Some other classes have a chance at least of temporary benefit from either an upswing or a downswing of prices; but the laboring man, handicapped economically and otherwise, is the most helpless member of society in the face of these conditions.

It is true that when prices are rising he usually finds it easy to get and keep a job, but he finds it more difficult than ever to get and keep a living wage. His money wages almost always lag very considerably behind the rising cost of living.

The most extreme instances of loss of real wages occurred in Germany during the early days of the great inflation which began in the middle of 1922. In one week in January, 1923, the wages of skilled labor of all kinds had advanced to more than 500 times the level of 1913. But the cost of living had advanced more than 1100 times; so that the workman's weekly wage of 18,000 marks would buy less than half what his weekly wage of 35 marks bought in 1913.

In fact, throughout the period of the great inflation there was a continuous Marathon race between the cost of living and the wage rates. In the later days of this period, wage adjustments in accordance with the cost of living index were made daily, but wages for both skilled and unskilled workers in all industries and occupations, except mining, continued to lag behind prices. (Wages of miners, because of the importance of coal in reparation payments, were given special preference, and in some months of 1923, notably April and August, the buying power of miners' wages was above the level of 1913.)

The height of absurdity was reached in December, 1923, when the average weekly wage of a metal worker was almost 30,000,000,000,000 (30 million million or 30 trillion) marks, or about 850 billion times the 1913 wage, while the cost of living had increased about 1,250 billion times. This metal working Crœsus with his pay satchel bulging with trillions of marks (truly "wealth beyond the dreams of avarice") was barely able to pay the butcher, the baker and the paper-shoe maker, since his 30 trillions would buy only about 70 per cent as much as his 36 marks would in 1913.

Higher wages, such as these German examples with prices ever going higher, are well styled by Edward A. Filene "counterfeit" wages. In so far as they pass for real wages, the workman is the victim of the Money Illusion. When he does partially wake up to the distinction between money wages and real wages his disillusionment often takes the form of blaming his individual employer instead of blaming the mark or the dollar.

When, on the other hand, the price level is falling the wage earners who are lucky enough to have jobs are helped by a reduced cost of living, but the hordes of the unemployed mean that labor, on the average and in the long run, loses by falling prices.

In short, labor loses in either event. The real wages of labor, as a class, are reduced, either by wages lagging behind the high cost of living (during inflation) or by some workers being out of jobs and having no wages at all (during deflation).

SOCIAL DISCONTENT

We have now seen two of the many kinds of harm done by unstable money: namely, the resultant social injustice, as shown in the last chapter, and the resultant irregularity in business, industry, and employment, as shown in the present chapter.

Out of these two economic evils arises another derivative evil, that of social discontent. The very fact that the people do not understand the change in the buying power of the dollar leads them to discontent. For instance, when inflation is going on and wages lag behind prices, the workman often thinks the employer is in some sort of a game to defraud him of every increase of wages by raising the cost of living against him.

An alienist who became interested in this problem remarked that unstable money seemed a sort of social insanity analogous to insanity in an individual. The individual who has an "unconscious conflict" does not know what ails him, but is restless and assigns the blame to the wrong cause. The public likewise do not understand inflation and deflation with their attendant evils, but do have a keen sense that someone is benefiting at their expense. The public therefore put the blame on the supposed rascal. When the price level is falling, the money-lender (the bondholder) is getting the advantage of the changing conditions and the public nickname him, as in the Bryan days of 1896, the "goldbug of Wall Street" or the "bloated bondholder." These, the banker and the money-lender, become the targets of popular discontent. When, on the other hand, the price level is rising the public blame and denounce the profit-taker and nickname him a "profiteer."

As we have seen, in neither case is the imputed blame by the public justified; the "bloated bondholder" could not help benefiting by falling prices and the profit-taker could scarcely help benefiting by rising prices. In 1919, a lumber merchant in central New York, not wishing to be called a profiteer, tried at first to charge for his lumber on the basis of arbitrary percentages, just as the Austrian bank figured the charge for the product of its paper mills. He suddenly woke up to the absurdity of the situation when he found that he was unwittingly selling his lumber, not to the public, which he was trying to save from "profiteers," but to the wholesale dealers from whom he had originally bought it! They found they could buy lumber of him more cheaply than they could get it from the lumber mills!

But, whether justified or not, popular discontent always follows in the wake of inflation or deflation. When the price level rises rapidly the laborers rightly feel themselves to have been victimized, and the more radical among them come to hate society. As inflation goes on, the workers grow continually more dissatisfied and attribute their plight to an intentional plundering by a social system of "exploitation."

Out of such discontent, therefore, come Bolshevism and other radical theories. Lord D'Abernon, during the World War, said that Bolshevism was caused largely by changes in the buying power of money. It is a crude effort to rectify what appears to be social injustice. And at least part of this social injustice is real, namely, that part caused by unstable money.

LABOR TROUBLES

Even the most reasonable workmen as well as the most reasonable employers are apt to get into disagreements because of unstable money.

Unstable money is, as Lord Vernon has well pointed out, a chief cause of bad industrial relations.

When the price level is rising the workmen complain, as we have seen, of the high cost of living and demand higher wages. This is a reasonable demand, but the employers are likely to resist, especially if they have a long-time contract or understanding with the workmen. A strike is often the result of the difference between these two viewpoints.

When, on the other hand, the price level is falling the employers try to reduce wages. This also is reasonable, but the workmen are almost certain to resist, especially if they have a contract or understanding to their advantage. A lock-out is likely to result.

As Lord Vernon puts it in his pamphlet on "Coal and Industry":

"If the dispute becomes serious the Government probably intervenes and holds an inquiry: the Sankey Commission of 1919 being an example in the first case, and the Samuel Commission of 1926 in the second. Eventually, either with or without a stoppage, but in any case after an immense amount of suspicion, misrepresentation, abuse and bitterness, the alteration of wages either up or down is made.

"This strange process is often referred to as 'making the necessary adjustments,' which really means the adjustment of wages upwards or downwards to suit the changing value of money, and it should be noticed that in the example given above the process starts in the first case at the retail end, when the miner wants to buy something in a shop, and in the second case at the wholesale end, when the coal-owner sells his coal.

"Neither party in industry likes the process. All sensible employers dislike reductions of wages and lock-outs, while workmen dread a strike. Both are, to a large extent, victims of circumstances over which they have no control, and if this analysis has any degree of truth it shows how childish is the feeling, which is so obvious in every dispute, about the words 'strike' and 'lock-out.' Both arise from the same cause—at any rate, in many cases—but the initiative is forced upon the workman in one case and upon the employer in the other."

It follows, therefore, that unstable money is one of the chief causes of industrial unrest, and stable money one of the chief hopes for industrial peace.

ALWAYS A NET LOSS

This study of the harm done by unstable money began with the observation that it makes our bookkeeping misleading, producing an unjust transfer of values from one class of society to another, but not, primarily, a loss to society as a whole. What some lost others have gained.

But we now find the losses exceed the gains, owing to the indirect harm of uncertainty, depression, unemployment, discontent, strikes, lock-outs, sabotage, riots, violence, Bolshevism. These can only mean a dead loss to the general public.

The loss is felt whether the price level is rising or falling.

When the price level is rising and business is temporarily stimulated, "prosperity" is largely a sham. Bondholders, most salaried men, many wage earners and all others whose incomes are fixed, or nearly fixed, in dollars are then far from prosperous. We must remember that "prosperity" is a business man's term, one that describes a condition of class interest rather than a condition of general welfare. It follows that, during inflation, the supposed "prosperity" of the period is really a class prosperity—an increased welfare of profit-takers at the expense of the welfare of others.

Moreover, as with ordinary gambling, even the gains of the winners are largely swept away in the end. When the price level is rising the strikes, riots and violence, which often occur, as secondary effects of the rising price level, take away the profits of the winners by blocking the wheels of industry and even destroying its tools. It is not so much a question of who is going to get the profits as it is a question of whether there are to be any profits. It does not seem too much to say, for instance, that, economically speaking, Germany probably suffered more after the War from her colossal inflation than from the War itself.

Similarly, when, during a period of falling prices, the apparent gainer is not the profit-taker but the creditor, the winner is also just as likely to lose his winnings. The bondholder is, usually and normally, the simple investor of capital, the "silent partner" in business. He lacks the temperament and training to be a risk-bearer or captain of industry. But, after years of a falling price level, during which he himself has been draining, unobserved even by himself, the life-blood of the enterprise whose bonds he holds, until there is no profit left for the captain of industry who has been managing it or for the stockholders who risked their capital, the mortgage is foreclosed and the captain, held responsible for the shipwreck, is forced out, discredited, humiliated, and unable to explain or even to understand that the disaster was not wholly his fault. The fault has arisen from his unreliable instrument of reckoning, the dollar. Next, the bondholders or their representatives, often lawyers, take control, whether or not they know how to run the business. Thus the management often drifts into wrong hands and turns into mismanagement. The bondholder has unconsciously been a Shylock, exacting his pound of flesh until the once productive enterprise is bled to death.

The workmen who are thrown out of work during a period of depression never regain their lost wages. Nor is what they lose gained by their employers nor by anyone else. Idle men and idle machines represent total losses to all society.

CONCLUSION

In this and the previous chapter we have seen that unstable money robs sometimes one class and sometimes another; that it upsets all sorts of calculations and economic relationships and adjustments; that it causes harmful fluctuations in trade and employment, and produces discontent, labor troubles, class hatred and violence;

and that in the end it represents general economic loss. These evils of unstable money may be reduced to three: social injustice, social discontent and social inefficiency.

CHAPTER VI

WHAT CAN WE DO OURSELVES?

CAN ANYTHING AT ALL BE DONE?

WE have seen the great harm of unstable money. But can anything be done about it? Must we accept the evils as dispensations of Providence or Fate, as we accept earthquakes and tornadoes?

Even earthquakes and tornadoes can be made less harmful by constructing our houses so as to withstand them. In this chapter we shall accept, provisionally, the fatalistic and helpless doctrine that monetary earthquakes and tornadoes cannot be prevented and that all we can do is to put our houses in order so as to withstand them.

As individuals have been slow to understand the evil which money does to them, owing to the Money Illusion, they have been slow to act for their self-protection. To rid our minds of the Illusion will help us immensely toward adopting a wise and practical policy in managing our business affairs. Many a man has failed in business from being oblivious to inflation and deflation and many have seen their opportunity and given a new meaning to Shakespeare's famous sentence: "There is a tide in the affairs of men which, taken at the flood, leads on to fortune."

TRANSLATING THE DOLLAR

One of the most obvious measures to take is to watch the quotations of the dollar's buying power and to use these figures for translating business accounts into a uniform standard. For this purpose, among others, I compute such an index weekly and publish it in the Monday newspapers.

This new and more accurate accounting can be accomplished without upsetting the ordinary routine accounting in terms of the dollar "as is." The new accounting simply affords supplementary statistics for the business executive and manager. The results will always be interesting to the executive and, when the dollar changes much, may prove a "life saver." The new accounting will often materially modify the figure for inventories and fixed assets carried at the original entries when the dollar had a different value. It may change greatly the figures for costs incurred in the past and alter profoundly the figures for profits, estimated and actual.

FORECASTING BUSINESS

Another use to be made of these indexes is to help, with other evidence, in forecasting business conditions. Any pronounced or prolonged fall in the price level usually foreshadows depression, while any pronounced or prolonged rise in the price level usually foreshadows improved conditions, from the business man's point of view. Of course, there are many other facts and figures, not related to unstable money, equally helpful in forecasting.

Another protection against unstable money consists in obtaining professional advice and warning as to the probable fluctuations in business conditions. Beginning with Brookmire and Babson, we have had, in America during the last two decades, an increasing number of agencies for this purpose with an increasing number of clients, subject only to setbacks when the forecasts were especially mistaken. These agencies afford statistical and, in some cases, forecasting services to business men in order to enable them, among other things, to provide against the evil consequences of inflation and deflation.

These business services now include, besides the bulletins from the Department of Commerce, the Standard Statistics Company, the Harvard Committee of Economic Research, the Alexander Hamilton Institute, the Karsten Forekastografs, Moody's, and other magazine services, the statistical departments of business houses and banks, and about 80 others. In England these examples have been followed by similar agencies, such as the service of the London School of Economics.

Herbert Hoover, Secretary of Commerce, has long been an advocate of such statistical helps, and they constitute, as we shall see, a part of the influence exerted by the Federal Reserve System toward stabilizing business. The Federal Reserve Board and Banks collect and distribute such information.

These modern business information services differ but little from the service which has been provided for generations by trade journals; but they usually lay more stress than do the trade journals on forecasting and on the measurement of general average fluctuations—the so-called "business cycle."

FORECASTING THE DOLLAR'S VALUE

Sometimes we can foresee clearly what will happen to the buying power of money. Then there is a rare opportunity to "make money." Foreseeing this impending change in money we can peer still further into the future and foresee the effects of that change.

Anyone versed, even a little, in economics and acquainted with the German situation after the War had a golden opportunity to make a fortune. Many in fact did, including Hugo Stinnes already mentioned. Some economists took advantage of the same opportunity, speculating in real estate, stocks, and foreign exchange, all on borrowed money. Such speculation was comparatively safe as long as it was known that inflation was still going on. It was obviously the part of wisdom, at such times, to buy no bonds payable in marks and to avoid depositing in savings banks. We have seen how badly those fared who lacked this wisdom—and they were the great majority.

The same principle, of course, applied and still applies in America. In the 1917–20 inflation some business men and economists in America deliberately followed these tactics of speculating on borrowed money, knowing that inflation was inevitable and understanding exactly what to do to make the most of it.

In the present day of comparative stability such opportunities are less and less frequent; but it is still the part of wisdom to be on the lookout for signs of coming periods of inflation or deflation, in order to avoid losses or to benefit by opportunities for investment.

INVESTMENT COUNSEL

When, as is usually the case, there is no telling which way the price level will go, some degree of safety may be found by investing in well diversified common stocks, with some preferred stocks and bonds as well. Such an investment is usually safer than investments in bonds alone, since the bondholder is really speculating on the future value of the dollar. If the dollar goes down he loses, while the diversified investment, on the other hand, made largely in common stock, is safeguarded. Since this diversification requires care and constant revision, the recent demand for diversified investments, as an escape for the investor from the unstable dollar, has led to the development of what is really a new profession,—that of "Investment Counsel."

One of these firms manages, or advises as to, investments aggregating some $200,000,000.

This new tendency to invest in common stocks seems revolutionary when contrasted with the older ideas on investments. Scudder, Stevens and Clark in their pamphlet *Elements of Investment Safety,* say:

> "In 1906 the Armstrong Investigating Committee of the New York Legislature, referring to life insurance companies, wrote: 'Investments in stocks should be prohibited. . . . Long ago the Prussian Government refused admission to its jurisdiction of any insurance company investing in stocks.' "

The book goes on to comment:

> "Following the committee's recommendation the Legislature enacted into law the policy which a little over a decade later was to stifle the German life insurance business after it had managed successfully to weather a most disastrous war."

Besides investment counsel, for advising the investor how to diversify, there is a rapidly growing list of "investment trusts," many of which do the diversifying themselves and give the investor a certificate entitling him to a share in the composite thus created.

CONTRACTING OUT

In times of extreme monetary instability in one's own country, while a neighboring country has comparative stability, individuals may partially escape by "contracting out" of the wildly fluctuating money into the better money (i. e., by buying foreign currency) or by making home contracts payable in foreign currency. In extreme cases the investor sells his own country's securities and invests the proceeds abroad. This was recently what the French investors did in their "flight from the franc," just as had been done a few years earlier by German investors in their "flight from the mark."

Contracts in foreign money, as Swiss francs or American dollars, were also made without actually sending capital abroad. Some German life insurance companies, in justice to their policy holders, converted their contract obligations into American dollars.

Contracting out was also practised in America during our greenback period, contracts being then made in terms of gold. In particular many bonds were made payable in gold dollars of the authorized weight and fineness. This proviso was revived about 1896, after a long fall of prices (1865–1896) had brought the subject into politics and Bryan had proposed silver inflation as a supposed antidote to gold deflation. Contracts were then made in anticipation of a possible debasement of the dollar in the event Bryan should be elected.

To this day millions of dollars' worth of bonds still have this "gold clause," but with no intimation of the conditions which originally led to the clause and in blissful ignorance of the fact that gold itself has already varied almost as much as the variation originally feared from silver.

Just as victims of paper money sometimes "contract out" in order to get the benefit of the more stable gold standard, so sometimes we find people seeking a better commodity than gold in which to express their contracts. In England tithes were often levied "in kind." In Scotland farms were rented in terms of grain, but the rents were actually paid in the money equivalent of the grain rent. This system was known as the "Scotch Fiars' prices." It lasted until a few years ago.

Jevons, the famous English economist, commended the wisdom of the founders of some of the Oxford colleges in providing that the rentals of the foundation land grants were to be paid not in money but "in corn."

Mr. C. W. Barron gives me an interesting example in the United States: "On September 8, 1817, David Sears, of Boston, leased to Uriah Cutting, of Boston, for 1000 years payable after the first day of December next yearly and every year during said term the yearly rental of 10 tons of First Quality of Old Russia Sables Iron . . . the land and building thereon at the northeast corner of Scollay Square and Court Street." Similar leases were executed at the time by the same parties on eleven other pieces of property. In each lease the rental was actually payable in money to be equal in value to the specified amount of iron.

In the central European countries, after the World War, it became the habit to make the contract for rentals, and even deferred payments of all kinds, in terms of commodities, usually wheat or rye. Such contracts existed in Austria and Rumania and other countries. In Hungary it was reported that bankers accepted deposits in Hungarian crowns, agreeing to repay the depositor not the number of crowns deposited but a number sufficient to buy the same number of bushels of rye as the original deposit was worth plus interest.

Such practices are prudent, and it would be well if they were more widely adopted. They not only protect individual interests but at the same time diffuse knowledge about the principles of stabilization.

THE TABULAR STANDARD

It is but a short step from such contracts in single-commodity standards to contracts in multiple-commodity standards. Under these the money payments are adjusted according to an index number, or, to use the earlier designation, according to the "tabular standard." An interesting example, and probably the very first, of the partial use of a tabular standard as a corrective for paper money instability is given by Professor Willard C. Fisher. In 1747, Massachusetts Bay Colony enacted a law in which a tabular standard was created for rating the bills of public credit. In 1780, Massachusetts passed a law providing for the payment of certain of its notes, both principal and interest, on a tabular standard. Notes were issued specifying:

"Both Principal and Interest to be paid in the then current Money of said State, in a greater or less Sum, according as Five Bushels of Corn, Sixty-eight Pounds and four-seventh Parts of a Pound of Beef, Ten Pounds of Sheeps Wool, and Sixteen Pounds of Sole Leather shall then cost, more or less than One Hundred and Thirty Pounds current Money, at the then current prices of the said Articles."

This action of Massachusetts anticipated the tabular system suggested by Lowe in 1822 and Scrope in 1833. Lowe proposed to establish a "table of reference" to be made up of staple commodities of general consumption, having regard to the comparative quantities consumed by the public. Mr. G. R. Porter, without mentioning Lowe and Scrope, proposed the same scheme in 1838 in his "Progress of the Nation." Porter actually constructed a table showing the average fluctuations of 50 commodities monthly for 1833–1837.

W. Stanley Jevons, in 1865, called attention to the fact that gold was not stable in value but had fluctuated violently between 1789 and the time of his writing, and in his book, "Money and the Mechanism of Exchange," 1873, he advocated a tabular standard of value to displace the widely fluctuating gold standard.

It should not be overlooked that Lowe, Scrope and Jevons were seeking a remedy for the fluctuations not of paper money but of gold. They anticipated in a great measure the idea of a more stable money standard which is being discussed today.

WAR-TIME EXAMPLES

The World War greatly stimulated interest in the use of index numbers for measuring price changes and fluctuations in the value of gold, so that in many cases, during or following the World War, a much more fully developed tabular standard was used, employing for the first time in history modern index numbers in a large way.

Labor in particular found a friend in the index of the cost of living, and used it as a lever for raising wages during inflation. Millions of workmen in America, and still more in Europe, have had and have now their wages adjusted according to an index of the cost of living. When the index goes up, wages go up accordingly. As Elma B. Carr, writing in 1924, says:

"The cost of living has entered as a factor into practically every award made by the Government arbitration boards. It also has been considered by

State and municipal agencies, and by State arbitration boards, and has been the controlling factor in the fixing of wages by minimum wage boards in 13 states and the District of Columbia. In the last 10 years it has entered into practically every industrial case which was voluntarily arbitrated. During the war, plans involving the use of cost of living figures were adopted by a great many private employers, and, while some of these have been abandoned, others are still in effect. Since the war many other firms have adopted definite plans for the payment of wages, all of which provide for the consideration of figures showing changes in the cost of living.

"It is impossible to estimate the number of employees affected by adjustments based on changes in the cost of living. The awards of Federal arbitration boards involved directly about 747,000 employees in the coal industry; 100,000 employees in the packing industry; 500,000 employees in the shipping industry; and 2,000,000 employees on railroads. In addition the awards of the United States National War Labor Board affected 711,500 employees in various industries.

"Since 1922, all commissioned officers, below certain ranks, in the Army, Navy, Marine Corps, Coast Guard, Coast and Geodetic Survey, and Public Health Service, have their subsistence and rent allowances determined by changes in the cost-of-living figures of the United States Bureau of Labor Statistics. This affects directly about 16,000 men. In the book and job printing industry of New York

City alone, the wages of approximately 22,000 employees were involved. In Chicago, in the same industry, the number of employees affected was between 9,000 and 10,000. The awards of the Council on Industrial Relations for the Electrical Construction Industry affect about 150,000 men. It has been shown that private employers engaged in various businesses have also utilized extensively cost-of-living figures.

"Altogether, the number of employees affected directly by specific wage adjustments is very great; those industries alone where the approximate number is known employ over five and one-half million workers. It should also be borne in mind that in many instances an even greater number of employees is affected indirectly, for often other employers engaged in the same character of work voluntarily make changes in wages, to conform to those fixed by an adjustment agency or granted by other employers. Therefore, practically all labor has been affected either directly or indirectly by adjustments which were based in some measure upon the cost of living."

It is of great significance that this application of an index corrective was made even in a gold standard country. The recent war period was the first time in history that there had been any such widespread confession that gold was a poor standard in which to make wage or other contracts and that such contracts needed to be corrected by an index measuring variations in the buying power of gold.

PEACE-TIME EXAMPLES

These wage adjustments flourished during inflation. They were popular with workingmen. But as soon as deflation appeared they began to be abandoned. The chief reason is that workmen, largely because of the Money Illusion, feel that any downward adjustment of wages lowers their buying power and object to it.

Nevertheless the plan of thus adjusting wages is still resorted to occasionally. The Philadelphia Rapid Transit Company, under the Mitten management, has recently introduced this system of a "market basket wage" based on a specially constructed Index of the Cost of Living in Philadelphia.

Occasionally other applications of the "tabular" principle appear. Mr. Frederick B. Knapp, in Duxbury, Massachusetts, lets his house at a rental varying with an index number. Originally this was the Index of the United States Bureau of Labor Statistics, latterly it has been my own Index.

A few years ago, the Rand Kardex Company (now merged in Remington Rand Inc.) issued a "stabilized bond" on the same principle. On it we find:

"The Company declares that it is its intention, by this obligation, to afford the holder hereof a steadier income in terms of real purchasing power than that obtainable from any other form of obligation, by providing herein for the increase or decrease of the sums of money payable hereunder when the purchasing power of the dollar falls or rises, in the sense that the index number of the prices of commodities rises or falls."

SUMMARY

We see, then, that even the individual can do something for himself to combat the harm which unstable money is always tending to do. He may translate his accounts into a more stable standard and thus find what profit or loss he is really making. He may make use of the recent behavior of money to help him forecast business conditions. He may make use of business services for the same purpose. He may, at certain times, forecast the behavior even of the dollar. He may avoid bonds as unsafe and invest in diversified securities, especially common stocks, instead. He may patronize investment counsel now being established for that purpose. He may "fly" from the unruly mark or franc and invest abroad. He may find other standards, including a tabular or index standard, into which he can "contract out" of the current one.

All of these things have been done, making in the aggregate many millions of instances of adjustments to counteract the effects of unstable money. They can be done still more, and doubtless will unless the measures discussed in the next two chapters are perfected sufficiently to make our gold standard really stable.

CHAPTER VII

WHAT CAN BANKS DO?

INTRODUCTION

IN the last chapter we saw that index numbers, by showing changes in the price level and in the buying power of the dollar, may be used to shield the individual from the effects of inflation and deflation by affording a means of readjusting contracts, especially those for wages, rents, and bonds. This use of the index number mends, or supplements, the unstable dollar, so to speak, by putting a patch on it from the outside. It has never been applied, and probably never will be, to the great bulk of contracts, both because it is too much trouble and because the Money Illusion prevents most people from seeing the need of it.

But instead of thus using index numbers for mending the dollar from the outside to counteract its fluctuations, they may be used for mending it from the inside to prevent its fluctuations.

To stabilize the buying power of monetary units has long been a dream of economists. And after the World War, with its new lessons in monetary instability, this dream has, little by little, approached realization.

Instead of resting in a monetary fatalism, some economists, bankers, and statesmen have come to recognize that nearly all inflation and deflation are man-made, and why should we not therefore have a man-made stabilization? We had already seen the need of an "elastic currency" by which the money loaned by banks should correspond somewhat with business needs. We are now seeing that we can complete that correspondence between the flow of goods and the flow of money by a better control of the flow of money.

There has come to be, since the World War, a more thorough and widespread understanding of the principles of money. It is being felt that a chief concern of workers, business men, bankers, and statesmen should be to secure the adoption of some preventive measures before the most recent sufferings caused by great inflation followed by great deflation fade from the memories of their victims.

Such progress toward stable money is now

easier than ever before because of the advent of index numbers. Only in the last generation has the Index been available as a tell-tale of the fateful fluctuations in money units. Just as we could not get a stable unit of weight until the instrument of measure, the weighing scale or balance, was developed, and just as we could not get stable units of electricity until suitable electrical instruments were developed, so we could not get a stable dollar until the instrument called an index number was developed. Prior to the advent of the index number as an instrument for measuring, even the concept of a stable buying power of money was too vague to form the basis of reform.

Instead of any such concept there was only the concept of fixed weight and fineness, the first crude attempt at stable money. When a stable weight was insisted on, it was, in fact, a great improvement over coins of different metal alloys, varying in weight and fineness, and over debased and sweated coins. But, of course, the only virtue in a fixed weight coin is that it is not usually so variable in buying power as an undefined weight or as irredeemable paper money, with nothing behind it to restrain a fall in its buying power. This partial improvement in value-stability is the sole benefit from having coins of fixed weight. The mere fixity of weight, of itself, has no other virtue whatever.

We have seen that the problem underlying the stabilizing of the dollar is to get a better correspondence between the two great streams, the circulation of money and the circulation of goods. This correspondence will not fully take care of itself even with the most "elastic" currency. But the correspondence is not out of our reach since the money stream is under the control of the issuers of money. The great issuers of money today are the central banks. They are properly expected to provide an "elastic currency" to expand or shrink with the expansion or shrinkage of the business to be done by it.

Under modern conditions, with our vast credit structure, the old theory of an automatic gold standard, beyond the reach of any voluntary control, has ceased to have much relation to reality. According to that theory, gold was supposed to derive its value chiefly from its use in the arts, and any credit currencies, such as paper money or deposits subject to check, redeemable in gold, were assured the same value as the gold itself. Any reaction which these "secondary" sorts of money might have on the value of gold itself was negligible. But today this very reaction is the main factor. Credit currency has grown to be a larger part of our money than the gold stock into which it is redeemable. In England and America, the proportion of credit currency to gold is about seven to one; the tail now wags the dog. Today, then, instead of saying that the paper dollar or the credit dollar derives its value from the gold dollar into which it is convertible, it would be truer to say that the gold dollar derives its value from the credit dollar into which it is convertible. And since the volume of circulating credit is controllable and controlled, we have already a managed currency in spite of ourselves. If we insure scientific management in place of hit-or-miss management, we shall thereby attain stabilization.

THE BEGINNINGS OF SCIENTIFIC CONTROL

At several international conferences following the World War the question of stabilizing the buying power of money was discussed. Finally, at the Economic Conference at Genoa in 1922, an epoch was marked by the unanimous adoption, by the representatives of more than thirty nations, of resolutions favoring such stabilization and indicating some of the methods to be employed. These included co-operative action among the great central banks of the world concerning the use to be made of gold reserves and as to the discount policy to be pursued. These economic experts, at the Genoa Conference, recommended:

"The essential requisite for the economic reconstruction of Europe is the achievement, by each country, of stability in the value of its currency."

They then proceeded to outline the specific steps which should immediately be taken, adding:

"These steps might by themselves suffice to establish the gold standard, but its successful maintenence would be materially promoted, not only by the proposed collaboration of central banks, but by an international Convention to be adopted at a suitable time. The purpose of the Convention would be to centralise and co-ordinate the demand for gold, and so to avoid those wide fluctuations in the purchasing power of gold, which might otherwise result from the simultaneous and competitive efforts of a number of countries to secure metallic reserves. The Convention should embody some means of economising the use of gold by maintaining reserves in the form of foreign balances, such, for example, as a gold exchange standard or an international clearing system."

THE ACTIVITIES OF THE FEDERAL RESERVE SYSTEM

Still more epoch-making was the inauguration of actual efforts in this direction by the Federal Reserve System in 1922. Officials of the Federal Reserve Board and Banks realized that, in America, with huge gold reserves threatening inflation, all possible steps should be taken to prevent it. Had they not taken such action but continued to follow blindly the profit motive, they would have loaned and reloaned their gold reserves until the credit structure had been doubled. Then the reserve ratio, instead of being, as it is, nearly 80 per cent would, under the profit motive, have sunk more nearly to the legal ratios—35 per cent for deposit liabilities and 40 per cent for Federal Reserve notes. This doubled credit structure would probably have led to a doubled price level, with a consequent inflation quite comparable to the inflation of 1917–20, and might have had as disastrous an end. Such a let-alone policy would not have safeguarded our dollar, but would have depreciated it, in spite of its fixed weight. Confronted with this prospect and with memories still fresh both of the disastrous inflation during and following the War, and of the even more disastrous deflation of 1920–21, the leaders in the Federal Reserve System instinctively sought to avoid repeating so shortsighted a policy. The previous inflation and deflation had given a rude shock to those complacent bankers who had thought money necessarily sound if only it was always convertible into a fixed weight of gold. It was also realized, perhaps dimly, that both the inflation and the deflation were largely the result of human discretion—in times of peace at least—and it was resolved that, in the future, such discretion should be more wisely exercised, in order better to serve the public interest. Then was born into the world a new policy, almost unnoticed and scarcely self-conscious, yet destined, I believe, to replace the traditional policy of drifting helplessly and hopelessly on the supposedly inevitable tides of money.

The dollar, in short, has been partially safeguarded against wide fluctuations ever since the Federal Reserve System finally set up the Open Market Committee in 1922 to buy and sell securities, especially Government bonds, for the purpose of influencing the credit situation. This Committee was reorganized in 1923 "with primary regard to the accommodation of commerce and business, and to the effect of such purchases or sales on the general credit situation." The Federal Reserve System thereby tacitly recognized its duty to control or influence credit, and seemed astonished, even a bit frightened, to discover that it possessed the tremendous power over credit which it has. This power, rightly used, makes the Federal Reserve System the greatest public service institution in the world.

The huge stock of gold and holdings of securities of the twelve Federal Reserve Banks enable them, in their dealings with the thousands of member banks, to buy or sell large quantities of securities in the open market, thus either increasing or decreasing the loanable funds of the member banks. When they buy securities they thereby put money into circulation. (It is true that it tends to flow out again if this new money is used by the member banks to liquidate debts to the Federal Reserve Banks. But this can be partially prevented by lowering the Federal Reserve discount rates so as to make such loans easier to carry.) When they sell, they thereby withdraw money from circulation. (It is true that it tends to flow in again through loans made to member banks by the Federal Reserve Banks.

But this may be partially prevented by raising the Federal Reserve discount rates so as to make such loans harder to get.)

Because of the reactions just mentioned—making or paying loans—there is closely associated with this Federal Reserve policy the further policy, mentioned in the above parenthesis, of controlling the discount rates. The thousands of member banks can lend to their customers the more freely the more easily they themselves can borrow of the Federal Reserve Banks; and the Federal Reserve Banks can make easy or hard terms by lowering or raising their rates of discount to the member banks, or rate of "rediscount" as it is called—according as circumstances justify the one or the other. Thus they can make the money we all use easy or hard to get, and thereby prevent inflation or deflation.

These two methods combined—buying and selling in the security market and the influence of the discount or interest rate—give the Federal Reserve System a powerful control over loans, prices and prosperity. Other methods are mentioned in the Supplement.

Some Americans are hostile critics of the "managed currencies" of Europe. They do not realize that our currency is to-day largely a "managed currency." The question at issue is not: Shall we adopt a "managed currency"? The question is: How shall our "managed currency" be managed? The Federal Reserve System does and should safeguard the country, to some extent, against serious inflation and deflation.

THE IMPORTANCE OF CREDIT CONTROL FOR AMERICA

Our prosperity has been looked on with pride by natives and with envy by foreigners, and almost as many explanations of it have been given as there have been onlookers. American genius and inventiveness, capitalism, labor efficiency, horse power, the "mechanization" of industry, democracy, prohibition—all these have been mentioned as factors in our prosperity, a prosperity which was maintained until the cumulative effect of a falling price level over a period of two years began to be felt. But the cause which is probably the most important of all, that is, stable money since 1921—approximately stable—has been all but overlooked. But it is no mere coincidence, I believe, that, of the ten periods in our history since 1849 mentioned in Chapter III, the tenth (1922–1928) has been unprecedented in prosperity and unprecedented in stability. In fact some of the other factors such as labor efficiency and contentment, scientific management, saving, and the mechanization of industry, have been made easier by the finer adjustments and smoother running of the industrial organization due to the greater stability of the dollar.

This factor has escaped general observation because of our old friend the Money Illusion. It is just as difficult to see and realize how the mere absence of inflation or deflation can produce prosperity as it is to see and realize how the presence of these conditions can produce adversity. In fact, it is even more difficult; for the absence of inflation and deflation will attract even less attention than their presence.

A most notable exception to the general failure to observe our new policy is found in the case of the Right Honourable Reginald McKenna, former Chancellor of the British Exchequer and now president ("Chairman") of the largest bank in the world. In the Midland Bank Monthly Review for January-February, 1927, he said that the Bank of England has survived for 80 years because the Bank Act of 1844, which is supposed to govern the credit situation, has always been suspended in time of crisis, so that credit may be better fitted to the requirements of business, instead of being, as required by the Act, arbitrarily restricted by the size of the gold reserve.

Mr. McKenna has proposed an inquiry into the "theoretical basis and practical technique" of the British credit and currency system, reminding his readers that, since the War, central bank reforms have been instituted in Albania, Austria, Chile, Colombia, Czechoslovakia, Danzig, Ecuador, Esthonia, Germany, Hungary, India, Latvia, Lithuania, Peru, Poland, Russia and South Africa. In all these countries, except India, not one central bank has copied the Bank Act of England; but, with that exception, all have adopted some system which is "similar to the Federal Reserve Act," which provides an "elastic currency," and, if properly handled, permits, as we have seen, the stream of money to keep pace with the stream of goods. While he compliments the skill with which the Governors of the Bank of England have operated under the old law, Mr. McKenna remarks on the greater elasticity of the Federal Reserve System as the main reason for the higher prosperity of America.

INTERNATIONAL CO-OPERATION

The Bank of England is already doing, however, so far as may be practicable, much the same things as the Federal Reserve System. Especially does the buying or selling of securities play an increasing rôle in the policy of the Bank. As Mr. McKenna says:

> "The use of the Bank rate in the determination of credit movements has been to a large extent superseded by what used to be its auxiliary, namely, open market policy—that is to say, buying or selling, lending or calling in loans on the part of the Bank of England."

The great central banks of Europe and America now hold informal conferences to discuss such policies and other matters of mutual interest. In June, 1926, such conferences, held in New York and Washington, were reported as taking place among a group of American bankers, Federal Reserve and Treasury officials, and the financial heads of France and Germany, looking to a recovered gold basis and stabilized price level for all Europe.

In July, 1927, the conference was again held in America. Among the subjects reported in the press on the authority of Governor Strong of the Federal Reserve Bank of New York as having been discussed were the "purchasing power of gold, and various proposals to promote closer co-operation."

Montagu Norman, Governor of the Bank of England, who took part in the conference, is, like Governor Strong, understood to be favorable to the idea that the central banks of the various nations should do what they can to prevent gold from becoming too cheap or too dear.

A third member of this conference was Charles Rist, Deputy Governor of the Bank of France. M. Rist favors the stabilization of gold, so far as may be possible, in relation to goods.

A fourth member was Dr. Hjalmar Schacht, President of the German Reichsbank. Dr. Schacht is the author of "The Stabilization of the Mark," and wrote an introduction to the recent article by the late Professor R. A. Lehfeldt of South Africa, in the *London Economist,* advocating gold-mine control to stabilize the buying power of gold.

These four men are singularly fitted to discuss such practicable measures to hold the buying power of gold stable as present conditions permit. If assurance of such stability can be attained, great price convulsions will be eliminated, to the incalculable benefit of practically everyone.

We may, it would seem, look forward hereafter to stabilization,—that is, the avoidance of inflation and deflation—as a conscious aim of the great central banks of the world in a form very much like that recommended by the Genoa Economic Conference.

There are two ways by which this stabilization work of the Federal Reserve System and other central banks may be perfected and more firmly established. One is by tradition, as the banks develop their own technique and extend co-operation with one another. It was chiefly through the force of tradition that the Bank of England gradually changed from a private to a public institution.

The other is by treaty agreements or "conventions" as recommended by the Genoa Economic Conference, and by legislation in the various countries concerned. There is now pending before Congress the "Strong Bill" aiming definitely to authorize and require a conscious stabilization policy, but leaving the Federal Reserve System a free hand as to how it shall be carried out.

THE INTERNATIONAL INFLUENCE OF THE FEDERAL RESERVE SYSTEM

Even without very active co-operation in Europe, the Federal Reserve System alone has a powerful reflex influence on price levels throughout the world. As long as other countries maintain the gold standard, any influence of the Federal Reserve System toward stabilizing the gold dollar carries with it, substantially, an influence toward the stabilization of the money of these other countries; for price movements in all gold standard countries will necessarily keep a family resemblance to one another.

Professor Bertil Ohlin of Stockholm has stated the case—in fact has considerably overstated it—in the Index of the Svenska Handelsbanken of Stockholm, No. 18, June 1927. He says that the movement of gold has lost all influence on the price level.

"The question of granting credit is instead determined by what the Federal Reserve Board considers suitable from an economic point of view.

"This implies nothing less than a revolution in the monetary system not only of the United States but of all the countries with a gold standard. The control of the development of the world price level has passed entirely into the hands of the Federal Reserve Board and Governors.

"Should that board deem it advisable to pursue a liberal credit policy, resulting in the raising of the American price level, the consequence would be that a portion of the superfluous gold would flow to other countries. There it would cause an expansion of credit and gradually a raising of the price level all along the line.

"If, on the other hand, it is considered in the United States that a reduction in prices would be advisable, then other countries are compelled to follow suit. Otherwise their price level would eventually be too high, their balance of payment would become 'adverse' and their gold would begin flowing into the vaults of the Federal Reserve banks. This the European central banks cannot, in view of their note-cover, permit, but are forced to carry out a restrictive credit policy that rapidly reduces the price level in Europe as well.

"Other countries are thus compelled to let their price level vary on about the same lines as the American. If the Federal Reserve Board resolves upon raising the value of gold, i. e., upon deflation, then its reserves increase, while, *vice versa,* a lowering of the gold value in the United States can be forced upon the whole world in connection with a reduction in the excessive gold reserves of the Federal Reserve system.

"The Federal Reserve system has effected a 'valorization' of gold, comparable to the Brazilian coffee valorization. By releasing a portion of the surplus reserves it causes a drop in the gold value throughout the world—i. e., a rise in the world price level. By increasing the reserves it brings about an increase in the scarcity of gold and a fall in the world price level."

This statement of Professor Ohlin, while fundamentally correct, gives an exaggerated idea of the Federal Reserve System's influence. That influence is far from being complete control and by itself never can be so. The influence of other countries on America is also strong. During the last two or three years, for instance, the deflation in England has probably exerted a strong influence to drag down prices in America. Any influence on credit reacts throughout the world.

But when sufficiently developed and co-ordinated, this influence of Federal Reserve and other central banks may grow into effective credit control, and when such effective credit control throughout the world is sufficiently reinforced by gold control, as discussed in the next chapter, we shall have approximated an effective control of the price level and of the purchasing power of money. Professor Kemmerer has said:

"Fortunately during the last six years, thanks largely to America's dominant position in the world's credit market, her enormous accumulation of gold, and the eminently wise administration of her Federal Reserve System in co-operation with central banks of other important countries, gold monetary units throughout the world have been moderately stable in value; but unfortunately there is little ground for hoping that all these favorable conditions will continue indefinitely. Certainly America cannot and should not carry in the future such large percentages of gold reserves for the benefit of the world at large as she has been carrying in recent years; the expense involved is too great for one country and likewise the responsibility. Moreover, the world's future production of gold is itself a great uncertainty. Will the production of gold increase more rapidly than the world's demand or less rapidly? This is a highly debatable question, but upon its answer will depend largely the future value of gold, and, if our present gold standard is continued, the welfare of literally billions of people.

"Within the last few years much progress has been made in the direction of a better understanding of the problem of currency instability, but the great problem of currency stabilization is yet to be solved. In my judgment it can be solved and will be solved."

CHAPTER VIII

WHAT CAN GOVERNMENTS DO?

RETURN TO THE GOLD STANDARD

WE have seen that credit control, even international credit control, is already in process of development. Such control must, in its details at least, be exercised by central banks, not by governments; these may only lay down general rules.

But there is much more than this that governments may and should do in order that we may at least possess a reliable monetary standard. First of all we may notice that the worst examples of inflation have come from unbalanced government budgets. As we have seen, when a government cannot make both ends meet, it pays its bills by manufacturing the money needed. Such issues of paper money have often been the chief source of inflation. When this is the case, evidently the first step toward stabilization must be taken by the government and must consist in balancing its budget. This was the great need in Europe after the World War. Without a balanced budget stable money is not a practical possibility. With a balanced budget it becomes possible to return to the gold standard.

Since the World War, the principal nations of Europe, one after another, have at last balanced their budgets and readopted the gold standard, or the "gold exchange standard," which amounts very much to the same thing. (Under the gold standard all other money is redeemable in gold; under the gold exchange standard it is redeemable in bills of exchange entitling the bearer to gold in another country.) A few, of which France is the most important, have not yet returned. The only practical road to international stabilization lies through the general return to the gold standard or to its equivalent, the gold exchange standard.

THREE WAYS TO RETURN TO GOLD

There are three chief ways of returning: the one used by Germany, of repudiating, or completely scrapping, her paper marks, already depreciated practically to zero by inflation, and starting all over again with gold marks; the one used by England, of raising the value of the paper pound up to that of the gold pound, achieved by deflation; and the one used by Italy, of lowering the weight of the gold lira to make it equivalent to the existing paper lira. These three methods might be called repudiation, resumption, devaluation. The first method, repudiation, worked injustice to creditors; the second, resumption, worked injustice to debtors; the third, devaluation, worked the least injustice, since the valuation of the lira decided upon was based more nearly upon its buying power at the time when the policy was put into effect.

Of course, the first method, repudiation, humiliates national pride. It seems a confession of bankruptcy or bad faith. Consequently, when possible, such a solution is usually avoided; the choice then remaining lies between the second and third methods, resumption and devaluation. As between these two, national pride will always prefer resumption, as it appears in the guise of a return to the original money unit, while devaluation seems to be a partial repudiation. The one seems to be a "return to normalcy" while the other seems to be the perpetuation of an abnormal situation. English business men took great pride in raising their pound sterling from approximately $3.70, its lowest value in terms of the dollar, back to the gold par of \$4.86⅝; while Italy gave up the attempt to raise her lira to the par of 19.3 cents and fixed it at 19 to the dollar, or only 5.26 cents.

THE PRE-WAR "NORMALS"

But neither country returned to the *real* pre-war value in terms of goods; for in terms of goods the dollar is only two-thirds of what it was in 1913, so that the English pound is, likewise, only two-thirds of what it was in 1913. Carrying further the logic of the Englishmen according to which the pre-war value was the normal to be aimed at, they ought to have raised the pound fifty per cent more than they did!

In neither sense, of course, was 1913 normal, any more than 1813 or 1713. The normal, if there may be said to be any normal, is always changing and always needs to be brought up to date.

The only sense in which the term "normal" can even formally be defended is that the government is bound, in good faith, to redeem its paper at the original par, and that it has the usual obligation of keeping a contract or implied contract. Of course our government would be derelict in duty if it did not redeem its paper money according to the terms written thereon. But when, as in Italy, or France, the government has already violated, and been forced to disregard, its obligations continuously for more than a decade, the situation is very different. The French or Italian government may, theoretically, according to the printing on its paper money, owe "the bearer" of each paper franc or lira a gold franc or lira worth 19.3 cents, instead of 4 or 5 cents. But the present bearer is not the one who suffered loss from the fall of the paper franc or lira from this original 19.3 cents to 4 or 5 cents. Hundreds of other bearers, predecessors of "the bearer" of today, have held these government promises, each for a few days or weeks, and the loss has been distributed among them. Restitution to them is now impossible, and it is sheer nonsense to think that the government, at this late date, can atone for such a long series of small injuries to many others by suddenly giving the amount in default in one lump to the present bearer. So far as he is concerned he would be getting four or five times as much value as he expects and as he gave when he acquired the paper yesterday from the last holder.

If to rob Peter to pay Paul is not justice, it is not justice to pay Paul what has been robbed of a series of several hundred Peters. We see then that, even technically, the argument for the resumption method on the ground of good faith is weak. The problem is certainly one of good faith but good faith in substance, not simply in form; and in that problem of substantial good faith the government's promises represented in its paper money are a trifling item compared with the great mass of contracts based, in good faith, on the confidence of the public in the paper money itself. Thus the government which uses the resumption method of getting back to the gold standard does not in effect keep faith with its public.

Italy attempted the resumption method and started out to bring the lira up from about 4 cents to 19.3 cents, but by the time about 5½ cents were reached by this forced deflation such trade depression and unemployment ensued that Mussolini wisely abandoned the project. Had he persisted almost all Italian business would have been plunged in bankruptcy and ruin.

France will be wise to give up any attempt at resumption and instead to devalue at or near the present buying power of the franc.

WHAT IS THE NORMAL LEVEL?

But what is the ideal level of prices at which to devalue? In general, it will be very close to the level of buying power existing at the time, for the reason that the majority of existing contracts have been recently made and are not of long standing, as well as for the further reason that, of those of long standing, a great part have but recently come into possession of the present holders. A railway bond may have been issued originally fifty years ago and yet its present holder may have acquired it only yesterday and on very different terms. Any change in the money of today can affect only this present holder and not those who before him have held the bond during the last fifty years. These earlier holders of the bond, like the earlier holders of paper money, cannot now be reached. Only a few of the original holders are still to be found among the present holders and we have no right to choose our standard to help the few and hurt the many.

Theoretically we could put a finer point on it by averaging the levels at which present holders of bonds and of other contracts or understandings in terms of money acquired them, but the practical result of such a calculation could not be very different from the existing level.

The truth is, once we have allowed inflation or deflation to occur, there is little possibility of curing the resultant evils. Even "farm relief," to cure some of these evils, seems impracticable. But, while cure is difficult, prevention is always available if only we could know it and would use it.

THE PROBLEM INTERNATIONAL

Whatever the method, the adoption of, or return to, the gold standard is obviously to be accomplished only by governmental action. The next question is: Has the government nothing further to do?

After the whole civilized world is again on the gold standard, the problem of stabilization will then be a thoroughly international one. The free flow of gold to settle international balances will then tend to equalize price levels among the nations. Each country will, or should, realize that, by the very act of adopting a gold standard, it has actually placed its national destinies at the mercy of the banking and governmental policies of other nations. What the dollar will buy in America will depend, among other things, on whether European nations keep the peace or go to war; and what the franc, mark, lira, or sovereign will buy in Europe will depend on the action of the Federal Reserve System. Scarcely any problem is more thoroughly international than this problem of monetary stabilization, because the action of any government or any great central bank affecting money in one country will affect it in all others having the same (gold) standard.

The gold standard simply puts in a connecting pipe joining together the money reservoirs of all gold standard countries, so that thereafter gold will flow freely back and forth and seek its level. Then English, American and all other price levels will rise together and fall together and the dollar, the pound and all other money units will fall or rise together in buying power. This international connection of all moneys will be the chief effect of having a common gold standard.

THE FUTURE GOLD PROBLEM

That standard of itself, however, affords very little safeguard against great inflations or deflations. In fact it may imperil the safeguards which, as we have seen in the last chapter, are afforded by credit control. That is, the gold standard, while it will help spread geographically the influences of credit control, will be in danger of hampering the power of credit control to stabilize. Unless governments co-operate with central banks, the credit control and the gold standard may be found working at cross purposes.

For example, if ten years from now gold should grow scarce enough to bring our gold reserves down to the legal ratios, further credit extension would automatically be prohibited by law, even if business required such further extension. The flow of goods would then outpace the flow of money, the price level would fall, and we would have depression of trade, unemployment, and all the other evils which inevitably come from any considerable deflation.

This is a real danger and one which is giving grave concern to such banking experts as George E. Roberts. One of the chief objects of this book is to help set bankers, business men and economists thinking in advance how best to prevent such a catastrophe as deflation or its opposite, inflation, by which such a flood of gold may come as to overwhelm any credit control.

Humanly speaking, deflation or inflation is sure, eventually, to happen, and the consequences are so economically disastrous that we cannot be too early in anticipating either event.

The truth is, as the reader may have inferred already, that such stabilization as we have enjoyed during the last few years has been the result of an exceptional opportunity. This opportunity was created by the existence of a surplus gold reserve, neither too large nor too small, but such that it could be disregarded. It thus provides a convenient margin or slack or elbow room within which credit control is unhampered. We have therefore had a managed currency, free within wide limits from constraint. Such an opportunity where we have a larger gold reserve than required by law, but not so large as to be unmanageable, never existed before and is not likely to last long or to come again. If we wish to make its blessings permanent we must see to it that the gold standard is made elastic enough to permit the stabilization of the price level through credit control. In short, the essence of gold control is to prevent gold from hampering credit control.

THE DANGER OF NEGLECT

The danger is that, instead of planning for gold control in advance of the need, we may trust to luck. This danger is great for three reasons: (1) the existence of the Money Illusion whereby most people are prevented from realizing that any such problem as guarding against deflation or inflation exists; (2) the belief that the gold standard should be kept automatic, that it should not be affected by any act of government; and (3) blind faith in the beneficence of this "old-fashioned gold standard" without the addition to it of any new-fangled improvements.

The first of these hindrances to a solution of the problem, the Money Illusion, is, of course, the theme of this book throughout.

THE "AUTOMATIC" GOLD STANDARD

As to the second, the idea that the government should make the gold standard "automatic" and unassisted by any legislative action, even if that implies (as it certainly does) unstable money, the reply is that there is no function of government more obviously proper than to keep stable the units by which we measure. We have a Bureau of Standards which fixes the units of length, weight, volume, electricity, and of every other unit employed in commerce, except the most important and universally used unit of all, the unit of value. Our Federal Constitution authorizes Congress to "coin money and regulate the value thereof, and of foreign coin, and fix the standard of weights and measures."

There is a popular fiction that our price level and gold standard ought to be left to the "natural" play of supply and demand and not subjected to "arbitrary" interference. Of course every unit of measure is "arbitrary." There is no "natural" yard. The gold dollar is already "arbitrary" at 23.22 grains. In fact it is *unnaturally* arbitrary to fix it in *weight;* for this interferes with the play of supply and demand on the price of gold. This price, on the plea of "naturalness," certainly ought to be as free to fluctuate as the price of silver, instead of being tied to the fixed figure $20.67 per ounce.

In the second place, the idea that the gold standard today is, or can be, "automatic" is wrong. As we have seen, gold is now far more influenced by banking policy than by its use in the arts for dentistry, gilding picture frames or making gold watches, rings and jewelry.

Such use is trivial in comparison with its importance in finance. As Reginald McKenna has said, the world now has a "dollar standard" fixed by credit control rather than a gold standard fixed by gold bullion as such. It is doubtful if Englishmen would have relished this fact had they fully realized it when they adopted what they supposed to be an automatic gold standard. For what they really did was to substitute for an English-managed an American-managed standard. They were afraid to trust the English government to manage its paper money so as to keep it stable but are now in the position of trusting the American Federal Reserve System to manage credit so as to keep it and all other money stable throughout the world. We already have human discretion, operating if not to control, at least to influence, the price level; we no longer have an automatic gold standard. And we ought to be profoundly thankful!

Only by the exercise of discretion, duly safeguarded, can we really expect some day fully to stabilize the dollar. When therefore the public understands the nature of the problem, the government will be compelled to do its part in safeguarding the dollar just as it does in safeguarding the yard.

THE GOLD TRADITION

To consider the third obstacle, blind faith in the beneficence of the "old-fashioned gold standard," let us see what history tells us. The modern tradition about the beneficence of gold was a product of the Napoleonic Wars and comes largely from the famous Report to Parliament in 1810 of The Gold Bullion Commission. This Report was the first really penetrating attempt at an economic analysis of changes in prices and rates of exchange in relation to money and currency. It showed, as might be expected, how the majority of the witnesses who appeared before the Commission were blinded by what is here called the Money Illusion. These witnesses imagined that the high price of gold bullion in terms of paper money was due to the scarcity of gold, because of the great demand for it to pay the armies in the Napoleonic Wars, "though increased also by that state of alarm, and failure of confidence, which leads to the practice of hoarding."

For instance, Mr. Pearse, then Deputy Governor and later Governor of the Bank of England, testified: "I cannot see how the amount of Bank notes issued can operate upon the price of Bullion, or the state of the Exchanges, and therefore I am individually of opinion that the price of Bullion, or the state of the Exchanges, can never be a reason for lessening the amount of Bank notes to be issued." After the testimony, the Commission asked Mr. Whitmore, Governor of the Bank, if he held the same opinion. The answer was: "I am so much of the same opinion, that I never think it necessary to advert to the price of Gold, or the state of the Exchanges on the days on which we make our advances. . . . I do not advert to it with a view to our general advances, conceiving it not to bear upon the question." Mr. Harman, another Bank Director, expressed his opinion in these terms: "I must very materially alter my opinions, before I can suppose that the Exchanges will be influenced by any modifications of our paper currency." The Commission then showed "That this doctrine [i. e., that there is no relation between issuing paper money and the price of gold] is a very fallacious one."

This bit of history is of interest as showing how the leading bankers of the day were not then staunch defenders of the gold standard but staunch defenders of the paper standard.

The Bullion Report expressed the most careful thought on the question of money supply and prices up to the time it was written and it still serves as an answer to the advocates of unlimited and unregulated issues of paper currency. But it was, at the time, a revolutionary document showing that the high price of bullion was really a low value of paper and that gold was a better standard than paper.

THE FIXED WEIGHT FETISH

That gold is a better standard than paper is today accepted as a matter of course. The banker and business man of today no longer resist this conclusion but some of them resist instead any advance beyond it. These seem to think that the gold standard is the ultimate end of all monetary developments. The Bullion Report represented the highwater mark of the stable money idea in the days of the Napoleonic Wars. But now, after the World War, we ought to go a step farther in stabilization by making use of the index number, a tool not available to the writers of the Bullion Report. By means of the index we can now set up a commodity standard, as great an advance over the haphazard gold standard as that was over the paper standard.

It was very natural, however, that, after the loss of the gold standard by European nations during the World War, the chief thought should be to return to it as far better than their paper standards, and the best with which they were familiar.

What then shall be done with the gold standard to prevent its restriction of credit control when the legal limits of the gold reserve have been reached, or when, on the other hand, there is a great excess of gold?

If the day comes—be it in ten or in fifty years—when all the margin, or slack, above the legal limit of the gold reserve is gone and no more credit can be built on the reserve then available, deflation will again come unless positive action is taken to prevent this evil. Or if the opposite extreme comes, when gold will become overabundant, inflation will follow unless we forestall it. In either case credit control will break down despite the best efforts of all the banks in the world. No wonder the Federal Reserve leaders shrink from assuming any responsibility for keeping the dollar stable.

We should then indeed relapse into the automatic gold standard with a vengeance; for we would have no power to determine where it would lead us. It would be the old hit or miss standard, a standard of chance.

PUTTING OFF THE SOLUTION

This evil day may be put off in various ways. The way which seems most definitely available at present, that approved at the Genoa Economic Conference, is to economize gold, that is, lessen the demands for it.

Gold may be economized in four ways:

(1) Gold may be withdrawn from circulation into the banks, especially the central banks. This has been done in Continental Europe, England, India, and other countries, especially since the War. It is practiced in the United States when gold certificates are retired from circulation and Federal Reserve notes are issued to replace them. The gold certificates are backed 100 per cent by gold; the Federal Reserve notes are backed only 40 per cent by gold. The withdrawal from circulation is helped if, as in England and India, gold bars are used and coinage stopped.

(2) Gold reserves may be concentrated in central banks as in the United States.

(3) The gold exchange system economizes gold, because the gold reserves kept on deposit abroad for the purpose of maintaining the currency at par with gold can be much smaller than the reserves necessary to keep in the banks at home in order to maintain the straight gold standard.

(4) An international clearing system would economize gold by obviating the necessity for most shipments of gold from debtor to creditor countries; just as a bank clearing house system in a city makes unnecessary most of the gold payments by debtor banks to creditor banks.

These four methods have already been adopted to some extent in Europe. Otherwise we might already be suffering from an international "scramble" for gold. Thus again do we find that the sound principles advocated by the Genoa Economic Conference are proving of great practical value, affording the beginnings of gold control, just as they have afforded the beginnings of credit control.

Most of the countries of Europe and South America which have recently come back to the gold standard, especially those which did so under the direction of the "international money doctor," Professor Kemmerer, have adopted the gold exchange system and keep their reserves in New York.

If, on the other hand, the opposite danger should loom up—that of an undue abundance of gold—the opposite remedy could be applied, the substitution of the straight gold standard for the gold exchange standard, thus scattering the foreign gold in New York among the respective countries which own it, or scattering gold from the few central banks to and among the many commercial banks; or scattering it from the latter banks to and among the pockets and tills of the public. At each such scattering more gold is required, just as, in the opposite case, less gold was required for each concentration.

This resource, of concentrating or scattering reserves, if properly used, is, and will long be, sufficient for our purpose. The idle reserves may then be enough and yet not too much to afford the credit control convenient elbow room.

Another way, or a special form of that just described, is to alter the reserve ratios in one direction or the other, even if this should ultimately make the ratio absurdly high—such as over 100 per cent—or ultimately absurdly low—such as less than one per cent. In the latter case we could not, of course, keep up the redemption on demand of all money based on gold. If the redemption, instead of being on demand, were on three months' notice, a much smaller reserve would suffice and the number of months' notice could conceivably be increased indefinitely, thus gradually dispensing with redemption in gold altogether. We may, in spite of all our prejudices in favor of the gold standard, be led to abandon it, either gradually or suddenly.

A leading economist recently told me of a conversation he had with some business friends who could not, as they expressed it, "see" stabilization. He said, "Well, suppose some German should make synthetic gold and make the process pay, or should succeed in extracting paying gold from sea water. They have tried both and failed. But if they ever succeed so that the world were threatened with a deluge of gold, making gold as cheap as yellow dirt, I put it up to you, what would you do?"

They replied that they did not know.

"Well," he went on, "I'll tell you what you would do. You'd see an emergency, and first of all you would get the governments of the world to close their mints to gold just as India closed its mints to silver in 1893. That would be stabilization. That is, it would prevent inflation. Then, when later, gold got too scarce you would open the mints again, but only part way, or decrease the weight of gold coin or do something else to prevent deflation. Stabilization is merely the prevention of inflation and deflation.

"Your justification for the gold standard is that it has safeguarded us from paper money inflation. As soon as you realize that it does not fully insure us against inflation and deflation of other sorts you will want to take whatever steps are needed to remedy the situation, even if you are forced to abandon the gold standard altogether."

POSSIBLE SOLUTIONS OF THE GOLD PROBLEM

But if we retain the gold standard even in an attenuated form, stabilization will never be secure until the gold base is controlled as well as the credit superstructure.

The most easily understood plan which has been suggested for gold control is one which has been proposed by several economists but especially by the late Professor R. A. Lehfeldt of South Africa. This plan provides simply an international governmental control of the gold mines, through, say, the League of Nations. A policy would be instituted such that when there is too little gold to support the credit structure required by the business of the world gold should be produced even if at a loss; while, on the other hand, when there is too much gold its production should be curtailed.

It is certain that an institution having the attributes of an International Federal Reserve Board could determine much more accurately the real need of gold for business than can the owners and operators of gold mines, actuated only by the motive of profits.

Another plan has been proposed by several economists, including myself in my book, *Stabilizing the Dollar.* According to this plan we would let gold production alone and merely change, from time to time, the weight of the dollar. Gold would then be left to follow its natural value so far as it does today, but the dollar would be preserved constant in buying power. Gold would circulate only in the form of gold bullion dollar certificates. A hundred dollar certificate would be redeemable in a hundred dollars of gold bullion at whatever the legal weight might be at the time of redemption. Periodically this weight would be changed, as prescribed by an index number, to make the buying power of the dollar always the same. Such a plan is called a "compensated dollar" plan, from the analogy of a "compensated pendulum."

This plan has been proposed in Congress through the Goldsborough Bill. Extensive hearings were held on this bill. A plan very similar, that of Mr. Tinnes of North Dakota, has been proposed through the Burtness Bill. The latter proposes (wrongly, I believe) *daily* adjustments of the gold weight of the dollar assisted by purchase and sale of government bonds.

These various plans are further discussed in the Supplement. It makes little difference which of the two plans, the Lehfeldt plan or the compensated dollar plan, as in the Goldsborough Bill, is selected or whether some other plan, more readily acceptable, shall be brought forward, so long as we attain our object, stabilization of the dollar.

The only alternative to gold control seems to be to abandon the gold standard altogether. We should then have to stabilize entirely by a "managed currency," as proposed by Keynes and others, or else by providing for redemption of all money in commodities. The latter plan has been worked out by Professor Gilbert Lewis of the University of California.

In at least three ways, then, we may meet the inevitably impending gold problem: (1) we may control the gold mines, operating them, as central banks are being operated, for public service instead of for private profit; (2) we may vary the weight of the gold dollar, or other monetary unit, in such a way as to compensate for the variation in the value of gold per grain, thus making the value of the dollar stable; (3) we may give up the gold standard altogether, either substituting redemption in commodities or relying on a managed currency.

THE GOVERNMENT'S RESPONSIBILITY

Any one of these three methods would require government action to effect. It is absurd to assert that while the government can establish standard and unvarying units of length, weight, volume, electricity and everything else we use in our measurements, it is powerless to establish a standard unit of value, in place of the dollar which now is merely a unit of weight. The weight of our dollar was fixed in 1837 but its value was left to shift "automatically," with every change in gold mining and our banking systems. The results, as shown above, have been tragic. When our statesmen once understand clearly these tragic consequences due to a changing unit for measuring values, we may confidently expect them to act promptly and decisively to remedy this defect.

If we can place the responsibility for our unstable dollar anywhere it rests on the government, not only in the sense of its neglect to stabilize but also even in the sense of its complicity in destabilizing. That this is true in war time will not be denied. Without debating here whether war time inflation can be avoided, except by avoiding war itself, we may point out that in peace time the government affects the value of money by every change in banking laws, and sometimes by affecting banking policy, or even by government finance. The government has an added responsibility when its own debts are involved. To borrow billions of dollars and then to depreciate the dollar is not even fair gambling. It is stacking the cards.

A further proof that government—national, state and local—incurs a moral responsibility lies in the fact that many legal provisions, intended to work for justice, presuppose stable money, and for lack of stable money, actually work injustice.

When I have urged on trustees, as in 1917–1920, to avoid investing in bonds they have answered that the law required it. Here then we find the government, intending to safeguard the property of widows and orphans, nevertheless compelling trustees to acts the effect of which is the exact opposite.

In times past, unscrupulous governments of kings and potentates would debase the coin of the realm in order to cheat their creditors. But the debasements wrought by modern governments, while evil intentions may be lacking, are far worse in the evil actually done.

We have already seen how in a trust account three-fourths of the principal was spirited away by inflation while in the eye of the law the principal was scarcely impaired at all. If only those concerned—the trustees, lawyers, legislators and beneficiaries—could see this clearly, they would be moved to laughter if not to tears.

And not simply trusts are involved; savings banks and insurance companies are subjected to legal restrictions intended to safeguard and protect, but which not only cannot do so without stable money but often actually do the opposite. Do not these acts of governments impose on them some responsibility to make their purposes effective and beneficial instead of injurious?

And likewise when the government fixes railway rates or public utility charges has it no responsibility for the actual effects on stockholders or public? The same question may be asked of laws fixing minimum wages, fines, penalties, licenses.

Lastly, attention may be called to the fact that governments aim to prevent the impairment of the obligation of contracts. Our own national Constitution expressly forbids the states to impair the obligation of contracts. It is true that the greenback decisions assert the technical right of our Federal Government to do so, but no one denies that it has no moral right nor that contracts in the greenback days were essentially impaired by our Federal Government.

The most elementary justice clearly requires that a government which specifically lays down the principle of justice in contracts, and which, intending to carry out that principle, regulates trustees and public utilities, prescribes rates, restricts investments and otherwise acts on the theory that stable money exists, shall make good on all these undertakings and not turn them into hollow shams.

No new constitutional provision is needed. We already have the provision that Congress shall have power to "fix the value" of money.

No particular theory of money is implied. Even those who do not believe in the "quantity theory" in any form will admit that every proposal described in this (as well as the preceding) chapter—with the possible exception of a managed fiat money—would at least tend toward stabilization.

No new principle is involved. We have stabilized every other unit as fast as we have devised instruments for measuring and fixing them. There is now no excuse for failing to stabilize the one unit left, the unit of money; for now we have the instrument for measuring and fixing it, in the index number.

We can at least make a beginning. Every other unit was crudely fixed at first. The yard is said once to have been the girth of the chieftain of the tribe and called a "gird"; then it was the length of the arm of Henry I; then of a bar of iron; now a fraction of a meter which is a length of a bar of a special metal kept at a constant temperature in the Bureau of Standards.

What would we think if today we were to go back to the "gird," if our yard were the girth of the President of the United States? What would we think if carpet dealers, in terms of a yard so defined, made contracts during the Taft administration and fulfilled them in the present administration?

Yet the injustices there involved would be negligible compared with the injustices we have suffered and seem destined still to suffer from our absurd yardstick of commerce.

SUMMARY

We may now summarize our findings:

(1) The problem of what to do about our unstable money is one of prime importance.

(2) It has been all but overlooked because of the Money Illusion.

(3) This Illusion is the more serious because every man finds it harder to free his mind of this Illusion as to the money of his own country than of foreign money.

(4) This Money Illusion so distorts our view that commodities may seem to be rising or falling when they are substantially stationary, wages may seem to be rising when they are really falling, profits may seem to exist when

they are really losses, interest may be believed to be rewarding thrift when no real interest exists, income may seem to be steady when it is unsteady, bond investments may seem to be safe when they are merely a speculation in gold. It makes a unit of weight appear to be a unit of value; it hides a chief cause of the so-called business cycle; it has enabled political financiers to employ unsound finance with burdens heavier but with complaints less than if sound finance had been employed; it has led to unjust blame of "profiteers" and of the "money lenders"; and above all it has held back stabilization by concealing the need of it.

(5) The present fixity of weight of our dollar is a very poor substitute for a fixity of value or buying power.

(6) By actual index number measurement, our dollar rose nearly four fold and fell back to the starting point again between 1865 and 1920.

(7) Most of the dollar's fluctuations were while the dollar was a gold dollar (1879–1922).

(8) They were largely peace time fluctuations; most of them occurred while America was at peace (1879–1898, 1899–1917, and 1918–1922), and much of them when there were no

important wars elsewhere (1879–1914 and 1918–1922).

(9) These fluctations, though serious, shrink into insignificance in comparison with the thousand-fold, million-fold, billion-fold, and trillion-fold fluctuations in Europe.

(10) The cause of a falling or rising dollar is monetary inflation or deflation and that, in practice, it is seldom or never necessary to specify that the inflation or deflation is merely relative since it is also usually absolute as well.

(11) To go back to the causes of inflation or deflation, the extreme variability of money is chiefly man-made, due to governmental finance, especially war finance, as well as to banking policies and legislation; but also due in part to discoveries or exhaustion of gold mines, and changes in metallurgical art.

(12) The tremendous fluctuations of money produce tremendous harm analogous to what would result if our physical yardstick were constantly stretching and shrinking but far greater

(a) because the money yardstick is used so much more generally,

(b) because it is so much more used in time contracts,

(c) because its stretching and shrinking are unseen.

(13) This harm includes a constant robbery of Peter to pay Paul—amounting to sixty billion dollars in six years in the United States alone—a net loss to all Peters and Pauls taken together, confusion and uncertainty in all financial, commercial and industrial relations, constituting much of what is called the business cycle, producing depression, bankruptcy, unemployment, labor discontent, strikes, lockouts, class feeling, perverted legislation, Bolshevism and violence. In short the harm is threefold: social injustice, discontent and inefficiency.

At this very moment unstable money lies at the bottom of, and partly explains,

(a) our western farmers' discontent, a chafing over their own deflation,

(b) the legal controversies over public utility rates as exemplified by the New York Subway 5-cent fare dispute,

(c) the French franc problem,

(d) the problem of England's depression and our milder one,

(e) the movement towards Investment Counsel as a new profession and Investment Trusts,

(14) We can, as individuals, safeguard ourselves in part against the harm from unstable money by translating our accounts into stable dollars, by trying to forecast the dollar's worth, by employing investment counsel, avoiding too many bonds, diversifying our investments, and by "contracting out" especially by employing the index as a corrective.

(15) The real solution is to be found in credit control and gold control.

(16) Some precedents for both of these exist, especially in the policy of our Federal Reserve System as to buying and selling securities and adjusting its rediscount rates, and the policy of European governments in economizing gold.

(17) Many economists and bankers are now studying the problem from a practical point of view.

(18) It is an old problem in a new form, the problem of insuring more exact standards of measurement. Only the dollar and the month remain still unstable.

CONCLUSION

The need of the hour is that those most concerned, business men and bankers, shall institute a study, or series of studies, on stabilization.

It may well be that the only methods available are already known but if so it still remains to select from among them the best and most feasible, and to decide what sort of index or indexes should be used in determining from time to time the value of the dollar.

These problems will never be wholly settled by academic men. The bankers and business men will accept only those policies in which they themselves have taken a leading part.

The object of this book is not to provide any cut and dried solution but to put it up to the reader, especially if he is a business man. Here is a problem of vital interest to you and one crying for solution. What are you going to do about it? If you reject every plan proposed, are you going to stop there, or are you going to take whatever steps are needed to solve the problem in your own way?

All that this book can or should attempt is to stimulate the wish to solve the problem. Experience seems to show that business men once converted stay so. As a friend expressed it, "once a stabilizer always a stabilizer." And on the fortunate few who see the problem and its importance rests a special responsibility to get others to see it.

The problem is one which applies to everyone. It applies to you who read these lines, especially when you save or invest, borrow or lend, insure your life, and plan to leave property to your children. It may mean the loss of your job or the wiping out of your profits. If you do not bestir yourself, and no one else does, this havoc-working, drunken dollar will remain with us always. It represents a great wrong which can never be righted as long as everybody leaves it to someone else on the theory that what is everybody's business is nobody's business.

We must transform this great duty of stabilizing the dollar from its present status of irresponsibility into a status where the responsibility is definitely fixed.

The crude beginnings of stabilization which we have enjoyed during the last few years are already worth much to you and me, adding much to the income of the nation, as well as safeguarding against individual injustice. We are all concerned to keep these advantages and win more. Stabilization ushers in a new era for our economic life.

Of course stable money will not be a panacea, a cure for all business problems, any more than the stable bushel basket was a panacea. Yet besides reducing social injustice, social discontent and social inefficiency, as already described, stable money will help indirectly in solving other great problems simply by making it easier to get at the facts, without any illusions. Before action upon alleged evils can be based on sure ground, it is essential to find out the facts; but the fluctuating dollar hopelessly conceals the facts. It blinds the eyes of the mass of men whose duty it ultimately is, under our democratic form of government, to choose one or more remedies for such evils as exist. The fluctuating dollar keeps us all in ignorance; whereas a stabilized dollar would lay bare the facts.

It is no exaggeration to say that stable money will, directly and indirectly, accomplish much social justice and go far toward the solution of our industrial, commercial and financial problems. There are, I believe, a few other reforms more important. But, among strictly economic reforms, it stands, in my opinion, supreme. When we really get stable units of money we shall have the greatest economic boon of all time.

SUPPLEMENT

HELPS FOR FURTHER STUDY

SECTION I

OUTLINE OF SOME PLANS FOR STABILIZATION

CREDIT CONTROL

CREDIT control must always be an important part of any program for stabilization. As has been seen, a start has been made in this direction by the Federal Reserve System. Some readers may wish to know a little more definitely what are the procedures employed for this purpose by the System.

The most complete account of what the Federal Reserve System is now doing will be found in a book by W. Randolph Burgess, Assistant Federal Reserve Agent of the Federal Reserve Bank of New York, and in the testimony of Governor Benjamin Strong of the same bank in the hearings on the (Congressman) Strong

Bill. Both books are listed in the reading list which follows.

Here, of course, merely the barest outline of the influences now exercised can be given.

HOW THE FEDERAL RESERVE IS OPERATED

The influence exerted by the Federal Reserve System is exercised in five chief ways:

(1) By buying and selling government securities through the Open Market Committee, organized to insure concerted action by the twelve Federal Reserve Banks (see page 132).

(2) By raising or lowering the rates of these Banks for rediscounting loans for the thousands of member banks (see page 134).

(3) By exchanging gold certificates (backed 100 per cent by gold) for Federal Reserve notes (backed only 40 per cent by gold) and the reverse, thus virtually putting the gold reserve into circulation or withdrawing it, at will. Such substitutions change the gold reserve ratio and, by that much, diminish the danger of its becoming so large as to lead to inflation or so small as to lead to deflation. As long as that ratio is comfortably above the legal ratio, yet not too far above, it may be disregarded in banking policy;

for within limits any change in it will have no effect.

(4) By moral suasion brought to bear on banks, especially member banks, thus tending toward concerted contraction or expansion of loans. This is accomplished through the contact men of the Federal Reserve Banks.

(5) By the publication of statistical information on the part of the Federal Reserve Board and Banks.

Of these five methods the first two put in practice what many economists have long since proposed. Alfred Marshall, for instance, in 1887 had shown the economic principles underlying the first method, together with many other suggestions for stabilizing money. The second method has been emphasized by Professor Cassel of Sweden in his *Money and Exchange since 1914* and by me in *Stabilizing the Dollar*.

GOLD CONTROL

Assuming that the gold standard is to be retained, credit control alone will not suffice to maintain a stable currency over long periods. Gold control is also needed, lest there be a conflict between the aims of credit control and the legal requirements as to gold reserve.

The plans for gold control thus far proposed fall under two main heads: (1) control of gold production and (2) control of the weight of gold in a dollar.

THE LEHFELDT PLAN

The first type is best exemplified by the plan of the late Professor R. A. Lehfeldt. He suggested in his *Restoration of the World's Currencies* that a syndicate of nations could control gold production:

"The syndicate would not even have to be a large one, for the British Empire and the United States supply more than four-fifths of the world's production of gold, and if they combined to regulate supply, even though the other producers stood out, the syndicate would be little more troubled than the diamond syndicate is by the river diggings. We put it this way to show how easy the syndication would be; but of course it would be far better to include all producers—Mexico and Russia are the next most important; and still better would be a truly international organization, for all countries are concerned in international commerce, and if the gold standard is to be adopted they should all take their share of the work of regulating it.

"To carry out such a policy of control, a Commission, appointed by the powers interested, would be needed. We shall not, here, discuss the constitution of the Commission, beyond remarking that the advent of the League of Nations should make it easier to agree upon; that, however, is not a matter of economics. Under the authority of the Commission there would be a scientific and an administrative bureau. The duty of the former would be to collect the information on which the decisions of the Commission were based. This would include: (1) monetary and banking statistics of all countries, (2) statistics of prices in selected markets, (3) information on the geology and exploitation of the known sources of gold, (4) information as to law and finance of gold-mining lands and the condition of mining companies. This work is well enough known to make it unnecessary to enter into further detail.

"The administrative functions of the Commission would be exercised, in the first place, through the intermediation of the constituent governments. No large staff would be required, unless the Commission decided to buy and work mines for itself. . . .

"The aim of the Commission would be to anticipate the changes of value, and correct them by intelligent action, instead of leaving natural forces slowly to stop and reverse the movement; that is, to play the part of governor.

"This aim might be accomplished in times of rising prices by closing some of the least productive mines, and preventing the development of new ones. Such a policy would involve paying compensation. The Commission would have to use funds supplied by the constituent powers to acquire such mines as it decided to close. There are many precedents for governmental action of this kind, and the government of the country concerned should facilitate it; but, as a mine whose yield is poor is of little value, the shares could be bought cheaply. When such action became necessary, the workpeople also should receive compensation; the Commission would do well to imitate the methods of the Swedish Government, in the case of tobacco factories closed on the establishment of a state monopoly in tobacco. It does not cost much to give compensation to displaced workmen during a period of unemployment, and much discontent is avoided thereby.

"It would be somewhat more difficult to arrange for new lands ready for development, but there is no impossibility in doing so. The Commission, or perhaps the government of the country, would buy ground on which the existence of workable ore had been proved; and might arrange a system of rewards for the discovery of new fields. In all this it would be making an investment of capital with a view to a future time when it will become necessary to encourage production. Of all the undeveloped fields at present known, the most valuable is the far eastern portion of the Witwatersrand, and as this belongs to the South African government, the problem of dealing with it is simplified.

"The life of gold mines is limited; a time of overproduction is followed by one of scarcity. For this reason the policy suggested in times of rising prices is not really expensive; rather it is a good investment. Later, when the production of gold becomes insufficient for the needs of commerce, the following methods would be open to the Commission to meet the scarcity:—

(a) Exploitation of land which the Commission had acquired, and on which it had suspended work. The Commission would be able to raise the capital needed for this.

(b) Encouragement of systematic exploration with a view to discovering new ore deposits.

(c) Encouragement of research into improved methods of extraction of gold.

(d) Facilitation of employment of paper substitutes for gold.

"The scheme outlined above deals principally with regulating the supply of gold: the possibility of operating also on the demand side is merely touched upon in the reference to use the paper substitutes for gold. It is possible that regulation of supply would not be enough and that it would be necessary to undertake deliberate action with regard to the ratio between the quantity of gold in use, and the quantity of paper currency of all kinds supported by it."

THE COMPENSATED DOLLAR PLAN

This is ordinarily referred to as my plan because it is set forth in most detail in my book, *Stabilizing the Dollar.* But only one feature of it was unanticipated by others, the proviso against such speculation in gold as might bring loss to the government treasury. As to the central idea, I was anticipated by Simon Newcomb, Alfred Marshall, and several others.

The arguments for and against this plan are given in the Hearings on the Goldsborough Bill mentioned in the reading list.

The main points in this plan are:

(1) To abolish gold coins and to convert our present gold certificates into "gold bullion dollar certificates" entitling the holder to dollars of gold bullion of such weight as may be officially declared from time to time. Thus gold would circulate only in the form of paper "yellow backs"—warehouse receipts for gold—while the only actual gold would be in the form of bullion bars in government vaults.

(2) To keep constantly a 100 per cent reserve of gold behind these certificates by issuing or retiring them as required when this 100 per cent ratio is disturbed by a change in the amount of gold in the dollar.

(3) To retain the virtual "free coinage"—that is, deposit—of gold and the free redemption of gold bullion dollar certificates. "Free coinage" would mean, as practically it means today, the unlimited purchase of gold by the government,

which would pay for gold bullion, as, practically, it does today, not in gold coin but in yellow backs. The only essential difference between the proposed and the present practice would be that the price of gold would no longer be arbitrarily fixed at $20.67 an ounce but would vary according to its real value or purchasing power. Likewise the redemption of the gold certificates would mean, as practically it does today, the unlimited sale of gold by the government—also at variable prices.

(4) To designate an ideal composite goods-dollar consisting of a representative assortment of commodities, worth a dollar at the outset, and to establish an index number for recording, at stated intervals, the market price of this composite dollar in terms of the gold dollar.

(5) To adjust the weight of the gold bullion dollar at those stated intervals, each adjustment to be proportioned to the recorded deviation of the index from par. Of course this is the same thing as adjusting, in the opposite direction, the price of gold.

(6) To impose a small "brassage" fee, say one per cent. That is, the government would charge, say, one per cent more for gold than it would pay for gold. The object would be to prevent the

sort of speculation at the expense of the government which would occur if, for instance, gold could be bought today of the government at $20 an ounce and sold back to the government tomorrow at $20.10. Each such announced advance or cut in the government's price would be restricted to the one per cent or whatever was the brassage fee.

The crux of the plan lies in the steering rule (No. 5) by which the index regulates the dollar's weight. Its significance is that, to keep the gold dollar from shrinking in value, we make it grow in weight, thus recognizing that a depreciated dollar is a short-weight dollar; and conversely, to keep the dollar from growing in value we make it shrink in weight, thus recognizing that an appreciated dollar is an overweight dollar.

The result would be that the Index, that is the price of the assortment of commodities constituting the "goods-dollar," would fluctuate but little in terms of the gold dollar.

When my *Stabilizing the Dollar* was written, I relegated credit control to the Appendix, assuming that all banking, even central banking, would still be conducted purely for private profit. My aim was to make the whole plan of stabilization—both gold control and credit control—as "automatic," that is as free from discretion, as possible.

Since that time, however, as has been shown in this book, discretionary credit control has actually come into existence. This, when duly perfected and duly safeguarded, will greatly simplify and improve the technique of stabilization and will make gold control secondary to credit control. A daily adjustment of the dollar's weight as proposed by the Burtness Bill would then be possible though unnecessary. But, without discretionary credit control, a daily adjustment would be disastrous. That is, if, as was my original thought, both credit and gold control are to remain "automatic," that is without discretion, so that credit control is secondary to gold control, adequate time (say at least a month) should be allowed for each change in the dollar's weight to exert some of its influence before another change is made.

At the opposite extreme from the "automatic," or non-discretionary, system proposed by me is one of discretion throughout so that, as has been privately suggested by two English economists, the Bank of England and other central banks should at their discretion change the weight of gold monetary units.

Dr. Hudson B. Hastings, a few years ago, who as researcher of the Pollak Foundation for Economic Research was detailed for eight months to study all proposed methods for stabilization, found the "compensated dollar" to be the only practical plan, not fiat money, for securing stability in the price level over a long period of time in any given country, which would work under virtually *all* circumstances and yet not compel that country to accept the sole burden of World Stabilization. He also stated that it was the most practical and least expensive of all plans for securing such stabilization by international co-operation.

But the compensated dollar plan has the disadvantage of being easily misunderstood, of confusing people by having the appearance of changing the dollar, rather than of keeping it from changing. It also seems more of a break with past precedent. The Lehfeldt plan preserves the present gold standard in form while modifying it in substance, a great psychological advantage in all popular reforms. Just as the British nation clings to the form of a monarchy while changing its substance to a democracy thus preserving loyalty to the King, though he has little or no power, so it may be easier, without dethroning King Gold, to keep popular loyalty to his standard by making it conform to a goods standard. Other arguments on both sides are considered in my book, *Stabilizing the Dollar.*

In the same book will also be found some discussion of the Gilbert Lewis plan of redemption in commodities, later set forth more fully by him in his article given in the reading list. If it were feasible, politically, to cut loose entirely from the gold standard tradition, the Lewis plan would seem, intrinsically, to be the best yet proposed.

In the text other means of stabilization have been mentioned such as varying the requirements for gold reserve ratios.

Another suggestion, made to me by a Canadian banker, is that if gold became so superabundant that the Federal Reserve System would have to lose almost all its earning assets (chiefly government bonds) in exchanging them for gold, the government should come to the rescue by supplying the System with fresh bonds, issued especially for this purpose, and taking over the gold itself. The government would then carry this gold as a dead asset, instead of the banks.

CONTROLLING THE FLOW OF GOODS

This book is devoted to the problem of controlling the flow of money. It does not deal with proposals to control the flow of goods except as, indirectly, that flow is affected by the flow of money. We have seen that the so-called business cycle is largely a "dance of the dollar" and that a more stable dollar will flatten out this cycle and go far to remedy the crises, depressions and unemployment from which we have suffered so grievously.

But it has also been pointed out that fluctuations in business and industry are partly due to other than monetary causes. Accordingly other than monetary remedies may well be applied. Were this book devoted to the "business cycle" in all its aspects these other remedies would require discussion.

Suffice it here to say that I am in sympathy—"in principle," at least—with the proposals of Foster and Catchings, Herbert Hoover, Otto Mallery, and others to further flatten out the cycle by so planning public works and business construction as to absorb any undue numbers of the unemployed. I am also heartily in sympathy with such efforts as that of the Dennison Manufacturing Co. so to plan business operations as to reduce the seasonal variations in employment. Finally, I believe that unemployment insurance is a very vital need in our industrial organization. These reforms would not interfere with but would supplement the reform here discussed of providing a more stable unit of buying power.

SECTION II

RESEARCH NEEDED

IT is clear that there are a large number of possible means available for use in any policy of stabilization. The best choice to make among these means, what other means, if any, may also be found and made available, and how we may best combine the means finally chosen are problems for future study.

Another vital problem is the choice of the best index, or indexes, to be used to guide stabilization.

For instance, should the index be one of wholesale prices, retail prices, cost of living, or the "general" index,—namely the index of prices of goods of all descriptions, including stocks, bonds, real estate, rents, freights, wages, and commodities both wholesale and retail?

This problem was the subject of animated discussions at joint meetings of the American Statistical Association, the American Economic Association and the Stable Money Association at Washington, December, 1927. The discussion was participated in by Hudson B. Hastings, of Yale University; Willford I. King, of the National Bureau of Economic Research; Miriam E. West, of the New Jersey College for Women; Carl Snyder, Statistician of the Federal Reserve Bank of New York City; Royal Meeker, formerly United States Commissioner of Labor Statistics; John R. Commons, of the University of Wisconsin; Ethelbert Stewart, United States Commissioner of Labor Statistics, and others, including myself.

There was much disagreement about which was the best index; but it was generally agreed that any index whatever was far better than none at all.

The "general" price index differs quite considerably from the wholesale price indexes of the United States Bureau of Labor Statistics. We have seen, however, that these two indexes, expressed in the form of purchasing power of the dollar in terms of pre-war cents, agree approximately. (See page 27)

Moreover, the agreement would be still closer if we had stabilization; for, the more wildly prices and their various indexes fluctuate, the more they differ among themselves; and the more stable are prices and their indexes, the more closely will they agree.

It is desirable, nevertheless, to choose the very best index possible, and, to achieve this purpose, further technical studies should be made.

Besides this question of the field, or fields, to be covered by our index, or indexes, there may be mentioned also: the problem of the best selection of samples to represent that field or those fields; of the best formula, including method of "weighting" (assigning the proportional shares of the various goods used in the index); and of the best base of comparison, or chain of bases. However, from a practical point of view, most of these questions may easily be settled by principles already established.[1]

Another problem is whether or not our index should be international and include representative goods of all lands.

A final problem is whether ideally the index chosen should be kept absolutely stable, or whether a gently rising or gently falling price level is more ideal. In particular, should the change in real income per capita have any consideration? Dean David Kinley once suggested

[1] See my *Making of Index Numbers* and "The Total Value Criterion, a new Principle in Index Number Construction," (Journal of the American Statistical Association, December, 1927).

that the best unit might be a certain definite fractional part of the nation's income. This would imply a slightly falling price level while important improvements in production were being introduced, which is most of the time.

All these refinements in detail are debatable questions. The main problem today is to get rid of the great fluctuations. The refinements can come later as we get the necessary data and knowledge to deal with them.

It will be seen that, while there is a wide range of choice of means and indexes whereby to stabilize, there is no general agreement as to which plan is best. Dr. Maurice Leven, through a questionnaire sent to economists, ascertained the present state of their opinion and reported his findings in a paper read before the Stable Money Association at its Washington meeting, December, 1927. He found that 252 out of 281 "consider stabilization of the price level to be a matter of major importance"; that 176 out of 262 think that the "general" index should be used, 59 that it should be the wholesale, 13, retail; out of 270, 88 favored the control of credit in some way, 70 favored the compensated dollar plan and 27 were indefinite, undecided or felt incompetent to judge, 53 knew of no satisfactory plan, 21 had miscellaneous suggestions and 11 were opposed to any plan.

What is wanted is the best practical program by which, taking the world as it is, with all its traditions and prejudices, with all the halfway measures already being tried, we may proceed, step by step, to the most ideal and most nearly world-wide stabilization feasible. The complete solution of this problem is worthy of the best efforts of economists, industrialists, bankers and statesmen.

SECTION III

READING LIST

SUGGESTIONS FOR FURTHER READING

The following list of 87 books and articles is selected from hundreds dealing with the subject of unstable money. It is representative of all shades of opinion.

Some on this list are for the general reader; others are more technical; some will be useful for following up quotations in this book. Each list is given in chronological order.

AMERICAN BOOKS AND PAMPHLETS

FISHER, IRVING. *Stabilizing the Dollar.* New York, Macmillan, 1920. xlix, 305 pp.

SCUDDER, STEVENS & CLARK. *Investment Counsel.* New York, Scudder, Stevens & Clark, 1922. 48 pp. New Edition, 1927.

STROVER, CARL. *Monetary Reconstruction.* Chicago, 133 West Washington St., 1922. 91 pp.

UNITED STATES HOUSE OF REPRESENTATIVES. Hearing [on the Goldsborough Bill] before the Committee on Banking and Currency of the House of Representatives. 67th Congress, 4th Session, on H. R. 11788. Pt. I. Pp. 1–125. Pt. II. Pp. 125–164. Washington, Government Printing Office, 1923.

BECKHART, B. H. *The Discount Policy of the Federal Reserve System.* New York, Henry Holt & Co., 1924. 604 pp.

SMITH, EDGAR LAWRENCE. *Common Stocks as Long Term Investments.* New York, Macmillan, 1924. ix, 129 pp.

CARR, ELMA B. Bulletin of the United States Bureau of Labor Statistics, No. 369. The Use of Cost-of-Living Figures in Wage Adjustments. Washington, Government Printing Office, 1925. v, 506 pp.

GRAHAM, MALCOLM K. *An Essay on Gold Showing Its Defects as a Standard of Value and Suggesting a Substitute Therefor.* Also a Translation of *The Death of Gold* by Gugliemo Ferraro. Dallas, Texas, Hargreaves Printing Co., 1925. 198 pp.

UNITED STATES HOUSE OF REPRESENTATIVES. Hearings [on the Goldsborough Bill] before the Committee on Banking and Currency of the House of Representatives. 68th Congress, 1st Session, on H. R. 494. Washington, Government Printing Office, 1925. 94 pp.

VAN STRUM, KENNETH. *Investing in Purchasing Power.* Boston, Barron's, 1925. 248 pp.

KEMMERER, E. W. Reports submitted by the Commission of the American Financial Experts.

Maps and charts. Report on the Stabilization of the Zloty. Pp. 3–48. Warsaw, Ministry of Finance, 1926. 364 pp.

DICK, ERNST. *The Interest Standard of Currency.* Boston and New York, Houghton Mifflin Co., 1926. 286 pp.

SODDY, FREDERICK. *Wealth, Virtual Wealth and Debt.* New York, E. P. Dutton & Co., 1926. 320 pp.

BURGESS, W. RANDOLPH. *The Reserve Banks and the Money Market.* New York, Harper & Brothers, 1927. xxi, 328 pp.

UNITED STATES HOUSE OF REPRESENTATIVES. Stabilization. Hearings [on the Strong Bill] before the Committee on Banking and Currency of the House of Representatives. 69th Congress, 1st Session, on H. R. 7895. Part I. Pp. 1–631. Part II. Pp. 633–1145. Washington, Government Printing Office, 1927.

AMERICAN PERIODICALS

NEWCOMB, SIMON. *The Standard of Value.* The North American Review, September, 1879. Pp. 234–237. New York, North American Review Corporation, 1879.

CLARK, J. M. *Possible Complications of the Compensated Dollar.* American Economic Review, September, 1913. Pp. 576–588. Cambridge, Mass., American Economic Association, 1913.

FISHER, WILLARD C. *Tabular Standard in Massachusetts History.* Quarterly Journal of Economics, May, 1913. Pp. 417–451. Cambridge, Mass., Harvard University Press, 1913.

TAUSSIG, F. W. *The Plan for a Compensated Dollar.* Quarterly Journal of Economics, May, 1913. Pp. 401–416. Cambridge, Mass., Harvard University Press, 1913.

FISHER, IRVING. *Objections to a Compensated Dollar Answered.* American Economic Review, December, 1914. Pp. 818–839. Cambridge, Mass., American Economic Association, 1914.

TINNES, D. J. *An American Standard of Value.* American Economic Review, June, 1919. Pp. 263–266. Cambridge, Mass., American Economic Association, 1919.

AMERICAN BANKERS ASSOCIATION. Report of the American Bankers Association Currency Commission on Dr. Irving Fisher's Plan to Stabilize the Dollar. Journal of the American Bankers Association, November, 1920. Pp. 239–240. New York, American Bankers Association, 1920.

ANDERSON, B. M. JR. *The Fallacy of "The Stabilized Dollar."* Chase Economic Bulletin, August, 1920. Pp. 1–16. New York, Chase National Bank of the City of New York, 1920.

SNYDER, CARL. *The Stabilization of Gold, A Plan.* American Economic Review, Vol. XIII. Pp. 276–285. Cambridge, Mass., American Economic Association, 1923.

FOSTER, WILLIAM T. AND CATCHINGS, WADDILL. *Business Conditions and Currency Control.*

Harvard Business Review, Vol. II. Pp. 268–281. Cambridge, Mass., Harvard Economic Service, 1924.

ANDERSON, B. M. JR. *The Gold Standard versus "A Managed Currency."* Chase Economic Bulletin, Vol. V. Pp. 3–39. New York, Chase National Bank of the City of New York, 1925.

BURGESS, W. R. *What the Federal Reserve System has done to our Currency.* American Bankers Association Journal, Vol. XVII. Pp. 599–601. New York, American Bankers Association, 1925.

BURGESS, W. R. *How the Mechanism of the Federal Reserve Prevented a Gold Inflation.* American Bankers Association Journal, Vol. XVII. Pp. 729–731. New York, American Bankers Association, 1925.

FISHER, IRVING. *Our Unstable Dollar and the So-Called Business Cycle.* Journal of the American Statistical Association, June, 1925. Pp. 179–208. Concord, New Hampshire, Rumford Press, 1925.

SHAW, A. VERE. *Elements of Investment Safety.* Harvard Business Review, July, 1925. Pp. 447–455. Chicago, A. W. Shaw Co., 1925. Separate reprint.

WILLIS, H. PARKER. *The Present Relationship between Credit and Prices.* Proceedings of the Academy of Political and Social Science, January, 1925. Pp. 111–131. Philadelphia, Pa., Academy of Political and Social Science, 1925.

FISHER, IRVING. *The Greatest Public Service Organization in the World.* American Bankers Association Journal, December, 1926. Pp. 438–440. New York, American Bankers Association, 1926. Separate reprint.

LOMBARD, NORMAN. *Judicial Salaries and the General Price Level.* Illinois Law Review, Vol. XXI. Pp. 312–315. Chicago, Ill., Northwestern University Press, 1926.

COMMONS, JOHN R. *Price Stabilization and the Federal Reserve System.* The Annalist, April 1, 1927. Pp. 459–462. New York, New York Times Publishing Company, 1927.

KING, WILLFORD I. *The Movement for Sound Money.* Burroughs Clearing House, October, 1927. Pp. 5–7, 44–51. Detroit, Mich., Burroughs Adding Machine Co., 1927.

COMMONS, JOHN R. *Farm Prices and the Value of Gold.* North American Review, January, 1928. Pp. 27–41. February, 1928. Pp. 196–211. New York, North American Review Corp., 1928. Separate reprint, 32 pp.

ROBERTS, GEORGE E. *The Gold Movement and its Effect on Business.* Forbes Magazine, February 1, 1928. Pp. 18–20, 40. New York, B. C. Forbes' Publishing Company, 1928.

STRONG, JAMES G. Speech in the House of Representatives, March 17, 1928. Pp. 5098–5103. Congressional Record, Washington, D. C., March 17, 1928.

HARWOOD, E. C. *The Probable Consequences to our Credit Structure of Continued Gold Export.* The Annalist. March 23, 1928. Pp. 523–4.

DUBRUL, ERNEST F. *Unintentional Falsification of Accounts.* National Association of Cost Accountants Bulletin, Vol. IX. Pp. 1035–1058. New York, National Association of Cost Accountants, 1928.

SATURDAY EVENING POST. Editorial, *Income Versus Purchasing Power.* Curtis Publishing Co., Philadelphia, April 7, 1928.

FOREIGN BOOKS AND PAMPHLETS

NICHOLSON, J. SHIELD. *Inflation.* London, P. S. King & Son, Ltd., 1919. iv, 143 pp.

CASSEL, GUSTAV. *The World's Monetary Problems: Two Memoranda* (for the League of Nations). London, Constable & Co., 1921. 154 pp.

CASSEL, GUSTAV. *Money and Foreign Exchange after 1914.* New York, Macmillan, 1922. vi, 287 pp.

BELLERBY, J. R. *Control of Credit as a Remedy for Unemployment.* London, P. S. King & Son, Ltd., 1923. 120 pp.

HAWTREY, R. G. *Monetary Reconstruction.* London, Longmans, Green & Co., 1923. vii, 147 pp.

LEHFELDT, R. A. *Restoration of the World's Currencies.* London, P. S. King & Son, Ltd., 1923. xi, 146 pp.

INTERNATIONAL LABOUR OFFICE. *Unemployment, 1920–1923*. Studies and Reports, Series C, No. 8. Geneva, 1924. 154 pp.

KEYNES, J. M. *Monetary Reform*. New York, Harcourt, Brace & Co., 1924. viii, 227 pp.

BELLERBY, J. R. *Monetary Stability*. London, Macmillan & Co., 1925. 174 pp.

GESELL, SILVIO. *Die natuerliche Wirtschaftsordnung durch Freiland und Freigeld*. Eden-Oranienburg bei Berlin, Freiland-Freigeld Verlag, 6th ed., 1925. 408 pp.

The American edition will appear in the course of this year.

KATZENELLENBAUM, S. S. *Russian Currency and Banking, 1914–1924*. P. S. King & Son, Ltd., London, 1925. 198 pp.

CANNAN, EDWIN. *Money, its Connexion with Rising and Falling Prices*. 5th ed. Revised. London, P. S. King & Son, 1926. 120 pp.

CASSEL, GUSTAV. *Das Stabilisierungsproblem oder der Weg zu einem festen Geldwesen*. (Tr. by Max Mehlen.) Leipzig, G. Gloeckner, 1926. 146 pp.

FUSS, HENRI. *La prévention du Chômage et la Stabilisation économique*. Brussels, L'Eglantine, 1926. 140 pp.

HARGREAVES, E. L. *Restoring Currency Standards*. London, P. S. King & Son, 1926. ix, 106 pp.

CANNAN, EDWIN. *An Economist's Protest*. London, P. S. King & Son, Ltd., 1927. xx, 438 pp.

FOA, BRUNO. *Influenze Monetarie sulla Distribu-*

zione delle Ricchezze. Naples, Societa Editrice Dante Alighieri di Albrighi, Segati & C., 1927. 146 pp.

LAZARD, MAX. *Rapport sur les Travaux de la Commission d'Experts Financiers Chargés d'étudier la Question du Controle International du Crédit.* Paris, Imprimerie Berger-Levrault, 1927. 28 pp.

OBLATH, A. *I problemi attuali della politica del credito.* Trieste, Industrie grafiche italiane, 1927. 190 pp.

PIGOU, A. C. *Industrial Fluctuations.* London, Macmillan & Co., 1927. xxii, 397 pp.

SCHACHT, HJALMAR. *The Stabilization of the Mark.* (Tr. from the German). New York, The Adelphi Co., 1927. 247 pp.

VERNON, LORD. *Coal and Industry, the Way to Peace.* London, Ernest Benn, Ltd., 1927. 40 pp.

HAWTREY, R. G. *Currency and Credit.* New York, Longmans, Green & Co., 3rd ed., 1928. vii, 477 pp.

MCKENNA, REGINALD. Speech at Meeting of London Joint City and Midland Bank Limited, January 24, 1928. London, Blades, East & Blades, 1928. Reprinted in the U. S. Congressional Record of February 24, 1928. P. 3683. Washington, D. C., 1928.

Also other annual addresses to the stockholders.

FOREIGN PERIODICALS

MARSHALL, ALFRED. *Remedies for Fluctuations of*

General Prices. The Contemporary Review, March, 1887. P. 371. London, Contemporary Review Co., 1887. Reprinted in Memorials of Alfred Marshall. Pp. 188–211. London, Macmillan & Co., 1925.

WILLIAMS, ANEURIN. *A "Fixed Value of Bullion" Standard, a Proposal for Preventing General Fluctuations in Trade.* Economic Journal, June, 1892. Pp. 280–289. GRIFFIN, SIR ROBERT. *Discussion, Fancy Monetary Standards.* Pp. 463–471. WILLIAMS, ANEURIN. *Reply.* Pp. 747–749. London, Macmillan & Co., 1892.

BOISSEVAIN, G. M. *Een Ideale Waarde-Standaard.* De Economist, 1913. Pp. 441–473. The Hague, 1913.

MARCH, LUCIEN. *Un Projet de Stabilization des Prix. Communication à la Société de Statistique de Paris,* le 15 janvier, 1913. Reprinted from its journal. Pp. 10–24. Discussion by Edmond Thery, G. Roulleau, Aug. Deschamps, Adolphe Landry, Lucien March, Irving Fisher.

ZEUTHEN, F. *Irving Fisher's Forslag til Prisniveauets Stabilisering.* Nationalokonomisk Tidskrift, July–August, 1913. Pp. 350–364. Copenhagen, 1913.

CASSEL, GUSTAV. *The Stability of the Gold Standard.* Quarterly Report, Skandinaviska Kreditaktiebolaget, October, 1924. Pp. 53–64. Stockholm, Sweden, P. A. Norstedt & Söner, 1924.

LEWIS, GILBERT N. *A Plan for Stabilizing Prices.* Economic Journal, Vol. XXXV. Pp. 40–46. London, Macmillan & Co., 1925.

CASSEL, GUSTAV. *The Shortage of Gold.* Quarterly Report, Skandinaviska Kreditaktiebolaget, October, 1926. Pp. 49–52. Stockholm, Sweden, P. A. Norstedt & Söner, 1926.

FISHER, IRVING. *A Statistical Relation between Unemployment and Price Changes.* International Labour Review, Vol. XIII. Pp. 785–792. Geneva, Switzerland, International Labour Office, 1926. Separate reprint.

FUSS, HENRI. *Unemployment in 1925.* International Labour Review, Vol. XIV. Pp. 203–231. Geneva, Switzerland, International Labour Office, 1926. Separate reprint.

MCKENNA, REGINALD. *The Transition to Gold.* Midland Bank Limited Monthly Review, January–February, 1926. Pp. 1–5. London, Midland Bank Limited, 1926.

CASSEL, GUSTAV. *The Connection between the Discount Rate and the Price Level.* Quarterly Report, Skandinaviska Kreditaktiebolaget, October, 1927. Pp. 61–64. Stockholm, Sweden, P. A. Norstedt & Söner, 1927.

D'ABERDON, RT. HON. VISCOUNT. *German Currency, its Collapse and Recovery, 1920–1926.* Presidential Address to Royal Statistical Society, 1926. Journal of the Royal Statistical Society, Vol. XC. Pp. 1–40. London, Royal Statistical Society, 1927. Separate reprint. 40 pp.

FUSS, HENRI. *Money and Unemployment*. International Labour Review, Vol. XVI. Pp. 601–617. Geneva, Switzerland, International Labour Office, 1927. Separate reprint.

HANTOS, E. *Die Kooperation der Notenbanken im Dienste der Konjunkturpolitik*. Bank-Archiv, 1 October, 1927.

MCKENNA, REGINALD. *American Prosperity and British Depression*. Midland Bank Limited Monthly Review, January–February, 1927. Pp. 1–6. London, Midland Bank Limited, 1927.

MIDLAND BANK LIMITED MONTHLY REVIEW. *The Course of Gold Values*. May–June, 1927. Pp. 1–6. *The Problem of Gold Values, Regulating Demand or Supply*. June–July, 1927. Pp. 1–5. *The Problem of Gold Values, National and International Stabilisation Projects*. July–August, 1927. Pp. 1–5. *Stabilising the Value of Gold, A Scheme of Anglo-American Collaboration*. August–September, 1927. Pp. 1–5. London, Midland Bank Limited, 1927.

OHLIN, BERTIL. *The Future of the World Price Level*. Index, June, 1927. Pp. 2–9. Stockholm, Sweden, Svenska Handelsbanken, 1927.

OSTERBERG, S. E. *The Standardizing Movement of To-day*. Index, No. 22, October, 1927. Pp. 2–9. Stockholm, Sweden, Svenska Handelsbanken, 1927.

TAUCHER, W. *Banknotenpolitik und Konjunktur und Krise.* Jahrbücher für Nationalökonomie und Statistik, January, 1927. Pp. 1–38.

CASSEL, GUSTAV. *The Influence of the United States on the World Price Level.* Quarterly Report, Skandinaviska Kreditaktiebolaget, January, 1928. Pp. 1–5. Stockholm, Sweden. P. A. Norstedt & Söner, 1928.

Other important articles on stabilization may be found in nearly all of the issues of this publication from 1920 down to the present time.

WIGGLESWORTH, F. *Gold and Stability.* Contemporary Review, April, 1928. Pp. 478–483. The Contemporary Review Co., Ltd., London, 1928.

SECTION IV

QUOTATIONS FROM OTHERS

SOME readers may be interested in the following quotations from other students and advocates of stabilization. They are taken, for the most part, from those collected and published by the Stable Money Association, 104 Fifth Ave., New York City.

Chamberlain, Lawrence. *The Principles of Bond Investments,* 1911.

"For loans of long duration there is involved in this matter of fixity of interest a more profound question than mere certainty and regularity of payments,—and that is the future purchasing power of the money . . . it would be better if the lender by any possible system of accounting could exact interest of so much per cent 'in present purchasing power of the necessities of life.' " (P. 17).

Mott, Howard S., Vice-President, Irving National Bank, New York, May, 1920.

"All violent, long continued or extensive changes in the general level of prices probably create more human misery than all other things put together."

Miller, A. C., Member Federal Reserve Board, at the joint conference of the chairmen and governors of the Federal Reserve Banks, Washington, D. C., October 26, 1921.

"We should seek just as earnestly to avoid deflation as we should to avoid inflation. By inflation I mean an expansion of credit that eventuates in a rise of general prices. By deflation I mean a restraint of credit that eventuates in a fall of prices. Good economic and credit policy will endeavor to steer a middle course between these two dangerous shoals."

Cassel, Gustav, *Money and Foreign Exchange After 1914,* New York, Macmillan, 1922.

"The only quality demanded of a monetary system which is of any importance for promoting the trade and general welfare of the world, is stability." (P. 254.)

"The maintenance of a practically fixed value for gold, however, is a problem of very wide significance. It is true that the value of gold, just as the value of all other commodities, is determined by supply and demand. But it would be quite incorrect to infer from that that we cannot exert any influence over the value of gold. Its supply must on the whole be considered to be dependent on the world's accumulated stocks of gold and on its annual production, which in its turn is in some degree affected by the purchasing power of gold, but is otherwise determined by natural conditions. On the other hand, we can exercise very considerable influence on the demand for gold—that is to say, on that important part of demand which is generally described as the monetary demand. . . . If for the future gold is to attain any stability in value, it is absolutely essential that the central banks should co-operate with one another in suitably limiting their demands for gold reserves. These demands must not be too small, but neither must they be too large; they must be constantly adapted on reasonable lines to the market situation, so that a practically unaltered gold value may be maintained. In future this will actually become the foremost claim on the gold policy of the great central banks. The very object of their keeping a gold reserve will be principally the stabilizing of the world's gold market which can be brought about thereby." (Pp. 263–264.)

Filene, Edward A., *New York World,* May 21, 1922.

"It may be that the stabilization of the purchasing power of the dollar along the lines advanced by economists will sometimes help to remove some of the problems of the counterfeit wage. A scientific solution is highly desirable. . . ."

Selections from Resolutions of the Genoa Economic Conference in 1922.

"The purpose of the Convention would be to centralise and to co-ordinate the demand for gold, and so to avoid those wide fluctuations in the purchasing power of gold."

Goldsborough, Hon. T. Alan, M. C., in the House of Representatives, May 23, 1922.

"I firmly believe that the purchasing power of money can be stabilized. I believe that the solution, when we have it, will be found to be simple; and I trust that that solution will soon be embodied in legislation."

McKenna, Right Honourable Reginald, Chairman Joint City & Midland Bank, at the Annual Meeting, January, 1922.

"The truth is of course that both [inflation and deflation] are bad. What is needed is stability, the point from which both alike proceed in opposite directions. When we have stability of prices we have a basis upon which trade can be carried on with confidence."

Iowa Bankers' Association in Convention at Ames, Iowa, 1923.

"It is the self-evident duty of the Federal Reserve Board to administer the Federal Reserve act in such a manner as will safeguard the Nation from the inflation and deflation in the future, and we heartily approve all sincere efforts being made to find and apply the best legislative method for safeguarding the purchasing power of money."

Snyder, Carl, Economist Federal Reserve Bank, New York, in *American Economic Review,* June, 1923.

"We should no longer have an appalling and endless number of strikes and wage disputes, and tie-ups and traffic blockades; for almost every strike and wage dispute grows out of a changing level of the purchasing power of money, and if this level of purchasing power can be made fairly stable, a large part of our labor troubles, so-called, will disappear. And with this would come a corresponding opening to all the talents of our inventors and discoverers and engineers and efficiency and production experts, giving them a wide-open opportunity to get at ways to enhance the man product per hour; to distribute the product more equably; to diversify and lighten human toil."

Strong, Benjamin, Governor Federal Reserve Bank of New York, in *Collier's Weekly,* 1923.

"Labor disputes are rarely very serious, long extended, or disorderly, except when they have to do with compensation, and compensation disputes almost always arise when prices are rising.

"Periods of falling prices give rise to demands for fiat money and Government subsidies of this industry or that.

"Therefore, is not the fundamental condition of industrial and national tranquillity that of a reasonable stability of prices, as from 1909 till toward the close of 1915?

"I believe with Mr. Henry Ford that what the great body of our workingmen most desire is security of employment and an adequate wage that represents a fairly even and stable purchasing power."

Zimmerman, Dr. Alfred, Commissioner General of the League of Nations at Vienna, interview reported in the press of October 29, 1923.

"Faith will return as the policy of inflation finally falls before a sound financial administration and stable money."

Alexander, James S., Chairman National Bank of Commerce, New York, in annual address to shareholders, January 8, 1924.

"—Although many believe that only with rising prices can prosperity be secured, true prosperity is dependent on stability."

Beckhart, B. H., *Discount Policy of the Federal Reserve System,* Henry Holt & Co., New York, 1924.

"The Reserve Banks were not formed merely to prevent money panics or to relieve autumnal tensions in the money markets, though both of these purposes have been realized. They were not organized to enable member banks to rediscount at a profit. They are not wholesalers of credit. Theirs is the function of promoting stability in prices and consequently in the economic life of the nation." (P. 538.)

Foster, W. T., Director Pollak Foundation, and Catchings, Waddill, of Goldman, Sachs and Company, in *Harvard Business Review,* April, 1924.

"The primary monetary need, then, is a stable unit of value; and this does not come by chance. Even if we had no other evidence, the records of the past five years in the United States should convince us that the country is not safeguarded against inflation by reserve ratios, or merely because bank credit is expanded 'in response to the legitimate demands of business,' or 'in the ordinary course of financing production.' . . . There are at least these four compelling reasons for taking measures now to make a dependable dollar the deliberate aim of conscious policy."

Keynes, John Maynard, *Gold in 1923,* The New Republic, Febuary 27, 1924.

"Currency reform has two objects: to remedy the credit cycle and to mitigate unemployment and all the evils of uncertainty; and to link the monetary standard to what matters, namely, the value of staple articles of consumption, instead of to an object of oriental splendor, it is true, and one to which Egyptian and Chaldæan bank directors attributed magical properties, but not otherwise useful in itself and precarious in its future prospects." (P. 11.)

Wolff, Dr. Frank A., Bureau of Standards, Washington, D. C., before the Committee on Banking and Currency of the House of Representatives, February 26, 1924.

"One of the greatest difficulties with which the Bureau of the Budget has to contend and over which it has no control is the evil of an unstable price level."

D'Abernon, Right Honourable Viscount, *German Currency: Its Collapse and Recovery, 1920–6,* Royal Statistical Society, London, England, 1926.

"There is a kind of ironical justice in the fact that the classes in Germany who in the end suffered the most heavy losses from inflation were those who were the most favourable to it in the early stages.

They imagined that loans contracted on a given date and repayable six months later in paper would be repaid by them on very advantageous terms, providing large note-issues continued to be made. They not unnaturally held that a currency dispensation which facilitated such a pleasant business could not be wholly vile or radically unsound. As long as currency depreciation remained within moderate limits their calculation was sound, but the final result was that, when the ultimate crash came, all the profits which had been acquired through this astute calculation vanished in the catastrophe, and the excessive issues which they had favoured led to the confiscation of so large a portion of their holdings that their temporary gains were more than swept away." (P. 38.)

Hoover, Herbert, Secretary of Commerce, *The World's Work,* January, 1926.

"What we all want from this economic system is greater stability, that men may be secure in their employment and their business—"

Rovensky, John E., *Installation Address* at the Annual Dinner and Meeting of the Stable Money Association, at St. Louis, Mo., Dec. 30, 1926.

"The most pressing economic problem of the immediate future is the stabilization of the purchasing power of money. This problem is world wide—more acute in some countries than others, but present in some degree everywhere.

"We view with satisfaction the more or less gradual return of the world to the gold standard, since it affords greater stability to money's purchasing power than any of the various expedients adopted during the war. But we clearly recognize that even a universal adoption of the gold standard is at best only a means to a return to the conditions that prevailed before the war. We shall have the problem of adding greater stabilization than that derived from a currency based upon one commodity—gold—and that commodity a metal whose production, distribution and use are subject to changes of tremendous importance."

Strong, Hon. James G., M. C., in speech before House of Representatives, February 20, 1926.

"The time has come, in my judgment, when the Congress of the United States, to whom is confided the exercise of the power 'to coin money' and to 'regulate the value thereof,' should declare for stability. Now is the opportune time in the world's history when the needed stability can be attained. We have nearly two-thirds of the world's gold and so can safely instruct for stability in the gold standard of prices.

"In 1913 the Federal reserve bill of Senator Owen

actually had in it a provision instructing the Federal reserve system to be so operated by its officials as to 'promote stability in the price level.' Furthermore, I am informed that this was written in the bill after it had been agreed to by the President and his financial advisors, but the World War was about to be fought and the time had not yet arrived for this great advance in the industrial and business world; but now the conditions are completely ripe in all directions."

Willis, H. Parker, *Presidential Address* to the Stable Money Association, at St. Louis, Mo., Dec. 30, 1926.

"The reform which is thus presented to the mind is of such importance that the utmost care should be taken to abstain from extremes of language in its behalf, and overenthusiasm or exaggeration of the benefits which may flow from it. Stabilization of the purchasing power of monetary units will not bring an economic millenium, but it should greatly alleviate some of the very serious evils which exist in the present state of instability. To show to the community how these evils originate, and to convince the citizenship of the country that they can at least be mitigated by stabilization, is the fundamental, the significant, task of this movement.

". . . I think we may truthfully say that there is a wider consciousness of the evils of fluctuating price levels and a more genuine realization both of the need of a remedy and of the possibility of finding it than there has ever been in the past."

Ford, John, Justice of the Supreme Court of the State of New York, December 15, 1927.

". . . For nearly half a century I have held the view that price fluctuation produced by faulty modes of regulating currency supply was one of the gravest evils of humanity and that it has been permitted to afflict the nations through a lack of understanding of the relationship between general prices and the volume of the medium of exchange."

Kemmerer, Professor E. W., at meeting of the Stable Money Association, December, 1927.

". . . the world sooner or later must either learn how to stabilize the gold standard or devise some other monetary standard to take its place.

"There is probably no defect in the world's economic organization today more serious than the fact that we use as our unit of value, not a thing with a fixed value, but a fixed weight of gold with a widely varying value. In a little less than a half century here in the United States, we have seen our yard-stick of value, namely, the value of a gold dollar, exhibit the following gyrations: from 1879 to 1896 it rose 27%. From 1896 to 1920 it fell 70%. From 1920 to September, 1927, it rose 56%. If, figuratively speaking, we say that the yard-stick of value was thirty-six inches long in 1879 when the United States returned to the gold standard, then it was forty-six inches long in 1896, thirteen and a half inches long in 1920 and is twenty-one inches long today."

Lazard, Max, *Rapport sur Les travaux de la Commission d'experts financiers chargés d'étudier la question du Controle International du Crédit,* September 14–18, 1927, Vienna.

"L'expérience acquise jusqu'ici révèle une coïncidence marquée entre la hausse du niveau général des prix et la prospérité, tandis que les mouvements de baisse coïncident plutôt avec les périodes de dépression. . . .

"Le pouvoir d'achat de la collectivité dépendant essentiellement du volume général du crédit, l'objectif proposé semblerait pouvoir être atteint en restreignant l'emploi des instruments de crédit quand l'indice des prix tend à monter, et en l'intensifiant quand cet indice tend à descendre. . . .

"La Commission estime hautement désirable que tous les groupements nationaux de l'Association s'appliquent à dégager les possibilités de mise en pratique dans leurs pays respectifs des principes ce-dessus indiqués, et s'efforcent, dans les limites de ces possibilités, d'en poursuivre l'application effective.

"Elle recommande que des démarches soient faites auprès des Gouvernements pour obtenir la nomination de Commissions officielles d'enquête sur le niveau général des prix, et sur les moyens de le régulariser."

Midland Bank Limited Monthly Review, "The Problem of Gold Values Regulating Demand or Supply," London, June-July, 1927.

"History has shown that apart perhaps from wars and religious intolerance no single factor has been more productive of misery and misfortune than the high degree of variability in the general price level. This may sound like an extravagant statement, but so far from being of the nature of demagogic outburst, it is clearly demonstrable from the course of events in various countries ever since money became an important element in the life of civilized communities. A stable price level is a thing to be desired, second only to international and domestic peace."

Pigou, Professor A. C., *Industrial Fluctuations,* Macmillan and Co., Ltd., London, 1927.

"I hold that, if a policy of price stabilisation were successfully carried through, the amplitude of industrial fluctuations would be substantially reduced —it might be cut down to half of what it is at present—but considerable fluctuations would still remain." (P. 198.)

Vernon, Lord, *Coal and Industry the Way to Peace,* Ernest Benn, Ltd., London, 1927.

"If it be true that the value of money can be moved up or down, then the methods by which this is done can be used to keep it constant within reasonable limits. . . .

"It is often implied, vaguely and mysteriously, that the central banks have the matter in hand, and that if it is left to the Federal Reserve in America and the Bank of England here everything will be arranged properly behind the scenes. Apart from the fact that pre-war results do not seem to justify this vague optimism, the idea that this represents is not only undemocratic but grossly unfair to the man-in-the-street, who has a right to know what is being done to the money that he works for and owns." (P. 29, 35.)

Warburg, Paul M., Chairman, Committee on Banking and Currency of the Merchants' Association of New York, May 24, 1927.

"The Association shares the view universally held that the interest of the country is served best by the greatest possible stability of price levels, and believes that in fashioning their discount and open market investment policy, the Federal Reserve Board and the Federal Reserve Banks should ever be mindful of this aim.

". . . It would be dangerous, however, to permit the fallacious impression to assert itself in the minds of the people that the Federal Reserve System (no matter how much its officers might bend their efforts in the direction of attaining price stability) could be held responsible for failure in attaining this ideal, which, as already stated, could only be reached by the co-operation under a common plan of forces entirely outside of the Federal Reserve System's control, not only in the United States, but all the world over."

Mellon, Andrew W., Secretary of the Treasury. Address before Chamber of Commerce of Charlotte, North Carolina, January 19, 1928.

"The nations of the world must be re-established on a sound basis, if our surplus products are to find an export market. Only in this way can business compute in advance the price which it must pay for raw materials and figure more accurately on the price which can be secured for the finished products. If this can be done, business can operate on a larger scale and increase its foreign purchases, which means a greater demand for our own surplus products and an expansion in business here and in other countries as well.

"It is indeed fortunate in this disturbed period in monetary affairs, when so large responsibility for world stability has been placed upon this country, that we have in the Federal Reserve System an agency capable, not only of exercising an important influence towards stability in our own money markets, but also of aiding in financial reconstruction abroad.

"The work which the Federal Reserve System is doing is along sound, constructive lines. But the greatest mistake would be to expect the impossible. It is not a panacea for all the financial and economic ills which may befall the country. Neither the Federal Reserve System nor any other system can control prices. The most that System can do is to influence to a limited extent, from time to time, the total volume of credit and its cost. While credit is one factor in influencing prices, it is neither the only factor nor the controlling one; and it would be asking the Federal Reserve System to perform the impossible if it is to be charged with the responsibility for controlling prices merely because it can exercise a limited control over the amount of credit available."

Commons, John R., "Farm Prices and the Value of Gold," *The North American Review,* January and February, 1928.

"Congress has given to them as a System authority for concerted action which enables them, as has been explained, to control the value of gold and the general level of world prices, but Congress has laid down no policy except the vague 'accommodation of business and commerce,' thus putting on the Federal Reserve authorities the unfair responsibility of using their uninstructed and private judgment as to what is needed by, and desirable for, the country from time to time. This omission has already caused a division within the System, as to whether the rate of rediscount should be uniformly lowered in order to help Europe buy American farm exports, or kept at a higher rate to aid the bankers in making profits. Had Congress retained the clause of the first draft of the Federal Reserve bill, which would have instructed the System to maintain stability of the general price level, the wholesome effect of a definitely known policy might have been enjoyed. Even the extreme fluctuation of 1919 and 1920 might have been avoided by stopping inflation sooner and making the deflation less severe, just as afterward a price inflation was stopped in 1923 and a price deflation was controlled in 1925. . . .

"This does not mean that stabilization of the value of gold would of itself change the spread between industrial prices and agricultural prices, or be a panacea for farm problems; but it would reduce the violence of future changes in the spread. A stable value of gold is merely stability of the *average* of all prices, and does not necessarily modify the ups and downs between *particular* prices which make up the average."

Editorial, Saturday Evening Post, April 7, 1928.

"This fact was the text of the harsh lessons received during the war years by thousands of persons who were living upon fixed incomes derived from sound bonds. Their coupons were cashed dollar for dollar and on the dot just as they had always been, but they were paid in dollars that had lost half their purchasing power. Incomes remained the same when measured in dollars, but when reckoned in food, shelter and clothing they were cut in two.

"So practical and so irksome was this lesson in elementary economics that we have a steadily growing third class of security buyers whose main concern is neither appreciation of capital nor stability of income, measured in dollars, but rather a steady flow of purchasing power."

Wells, H. G., *Has the Money-Credit System a Mind?* The Saturday Evening Post, May 5, 1928.

"Three main things the world requires from its money-credit organization. The first is trustworthy wages. By that is meant a payment for a day's work, a week's work, or a month's work, that will surely keep its promise to the worker. It must represent absolutely stable purchasing power. It must never evaporate. If the worker chooses to hold his wages for a time and then buy, he must find that they can still buy what he reckoned to get when he earned them. When money will give that full assurance, the worker will work his best. So far as it fails to do that, his irritation and demoralization will develop. . . . And next to this question of security of payment, in pursuit of this problem of a happy and productive humanity, is the question of security of employment."

Views of one hundred British Industrialists, New York Times, May 27, 1928.

"The ills of British industry are not due to high taxes but to the present monetary system, according to the belief of one hundred men associated with productive industries who have sent Prime Minister Baldwin a letter on the subject. The list includes such names as that of Sir Auckland Geddes, former Ambassador to the United States, and Lord Denbigh.

"Proposing their solution for industry's ills, the signatories say: 'We believe that a more stable system of currency credit and a means of stabilizing the price level are pre-requisite to the restoration of prosperity of the great basic industries of the country. It would do far more than the expedients which the Government has been compelled to adopt.' "

INDEX